SRA

ART

Connections

Artist Profiles

Columbus, OH

The **McGraw·Hill** Companies

Photo Credits

SRAonline.com

Table of Contents

Adams, Ansel 3

Ashoona, Kiawak 4

Audubon, John James 5

Beaux, Cecilia 6

Bell, John 7

Benton, Thomas Hart 8

Brach, Paul 9

Catlin, George 10

Cézanne, Paul 11

Chryssa 12

Cordero, Helen 13

Degas, Edgar 14

Delaunay, Robert 15

Dentzel Company 16

Des Jarlait, Patrick 17

Diebenkorn, Richard 18

Eyre, Ivan 19

Gay, Jacob 20

Gottlieb, Adolph 21

Hanson, Duane 22

Herbin, Auguste 23

Hockney, David 24

Hopper, Edward 25

Jacquette, Yvonne 26

Johnson, Willam H. 27

Kandinsky, Wassily 28

Kensett, John Frederick 29

Klee, Paul 30

Kline, Franz 31

Lawrence, Jacob 32

Lionni, Leo 33

Lostutter, Robert 34

Magritte, René 35

McCloskey, William 36

Mendoza, Herón Martínez 37

Merian, Maria Sibylla 38

Moillon, Louise 39

Monet, Claude 40

Moore, Henry 41

Moroles, Jesús 42

Grandma Moses 43
Nevelson, Louise 44
Nuna, Taqialuk 45
O´Keeffe, Georgia 46
Peale, James 47
Ragans, Rosalind 48
Renoir, Pierre Auguste 49
Rodia, Simon 50
Schapiro, Miriam 51
Schimmel, Wilhelm 52
Scott, John 53
Scott, Lorenzo 54
Shannon, James J. 55
Smith, David 56
Steichen, Edward 57
Stella, Joseph 58
Swentzell, Roxanne 59
Teichert, Minerva 60
Thomson, Tom 61
Town, Harold 62
Twiggs, Leo 63
van Gogh, Vincent 64
Van Ness, Beatrice Whitney 65
van Rijn, Rembrandt 66
Velázquez, Diego 67
Vermeer, Jan 68
Wilson, Jane 69
Yoruba Headdress 70
Zalucha, Peggy Flora 71
Delaware Shoulder Bag 72
Gui Ritual Food Container 73
Indonesian Shadow Puppet 74
Leopard Aquamanile 75
Lekythos 76
Maison Carrée 77
Map Quilt 78
Pectoral with the Name of Senwosret II 79
Plate with King Hunting Rams 80
Princess Feather and Rising Sun Quilt 81
Pueblo Scene: Corn Dancers and Church 82
Shadow Puppet 83

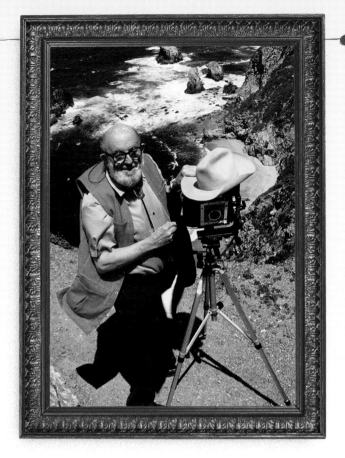

▲ **Ansel Adams.** (American). *Self-Portrait.*

Silver gelatin print.

Ansel Adams
1902–1984

Ansel Adams (an´ səl ad´ əms) was born in San Francisco. In 1903, his family moved to a house amid the sand dunes near the ocean. Adams always believed that the sights, sounds, and smells of the ocean shaped the way he thought. Adams had a difficult time at school. With his father's approval, he quit early, intending to become a classical pianist. He became fascinated with the beauty of places such as the Yosemite valley, but was frustrated that his photography did not catch its inherent grandeur. As he pursued perfecting his photographic and development processes his talent became evident to others, and books containing his photographs began to sell. His popularity continued to increase, even after his death in 1984.

About Art History

Georgia O'Keeffe's husband, Alfred Stieglitz, had a small gallery in New York City called An American Place. He gave Adams a show of his own in 1936. Stieglitz was an important advocate for both O'Keeffe and Adams. He also displayed the photography of Paul Strand and the paintings of John Marin.

About the Artwork

Adams wanted to share his appreciation of nature through his photography. He was a member of the Sierra Club and worked for that organization toward the preservation and appreciation of natural resources. Adams constantly experimented with materials and techniques to create the finest prints possible. He printed his photograph *Moonrise, Hernandez,* taken in 1941, more than 1,300 times, and finally felt he got it right in the 1970s.

About the Media

Adams began taking photographs on a Kodak Box Brownie camera in 1916. He tried many cameras over the years, even an instant Polaroid. He did some work with color in the mid-1940s, but because color photographs fade over time, he preferred to work in black and white.

About the Technique

Before he took a photograph, Adams visualized the scene, recorded the camera settings, and took notes about the process. Adams felt that his darkroom ability was as important as his photographic ability. He made gelatin silver prints, which are papers coated with gelatin that contains light-sensitive silver salts. They were developed in the 1870s and had the advantage of not turning yellow and being simpler to produce. Gelatin silver prints remain the standard black-and-white print type.

Kiawak Ashoona

b. 1933

Kiawak Ashoona (kē ə wak ə shoo nə) was born and grew up on the Eastern Arctic's Cape Dorset, Nunuvut, in northern Canada. His sculptural skills were self-taught, and he is one of the last remaining members of the original generation of Inuit artists. In fact, Inuit art received some of its earliest attention and appreciation because of Ashoona's individual and detailed style. Over the years his work has been given as gifts to foreign dignitaries, exhibited in galleries across the world, and replicated on a Canadian postage stamp. New generations of artists respect Ashoona's technique and imagination and have followed his lead in both innovative and traditional Inuit carving styles.

About Art History

Ashoona began his artistic career when he was a boy. In order to survive after his father died, Ashoona's family had to work very hard, so he started to carve to create artwork to sell. Soon he was carving and trading on a regular basis. He still considers his artistry a means of carrying on the tradition of his community. The Inuit population is widely distributed across northern Canada, and each of the 30 art-producing communities specializes in its own favorite subjects and sculptural style. Each artist takes an individual approach, ranging from naturalism or decorative stylization to minimal abstraction or surrealism.

About the Artwork

Ashoona's art can be identified by its intricate attention to detail. Fantastic creatures of Inuit mythology and Ashoona's imagination appear on his carved sculptures. Themes of arctic wildlife, traditional Inuit hunting and family scenes, spirit figures and mythological and shamanistic figures are popular in much of his carving. *Seal Hunter* depicts a young, content hunter with his spear.

The smooth finish and facial detail of the sculpture are characteristic of Ashoona's style.

About the Media

Rock from the arctic area is often worked into Ashoona's sculpture. The predominantly gray stones are usually blackened and polished and then incised or carved. *Seal Hunter* was made from green serpentine, a kind of dark green rock that looks like marble.

About the Technique

Ashoona works with a reduction method. His sculptures begin as blocks of stone that he slowly carves away to form smooth, sleek forms. Chisels, blades, and sanding stones are used to shape and define his work.

John James Audubon
1785–1851

John James Audubon (jän jāmz ô´ də bən) was born in Santo Domingo, now Haiti. His mother died a few months after he was born, so he was raised in France by his father and his father's wife, a kind woman who encouraged his love of the outdoors and art. When he was 18, he left France for America to live on one of his father's plantations in Pennsylvania. Audubon drew birds only as a hobby until he and his family met with hard financial times. Audubon's successful journeys established him as a leading romantic painter and expert on ornithology. Years after his death the National Audubon Society was founded in his name.

About Art History

At age 18, Audubon arrived in Pennsylvania to live on his father's estate and escape conscription into Napoleon's army. He had a comfortable business career until 1819, when he was briefly jailed for bankruptcy and forced to seek prospects elsewhere. Sailing down the Mississippi, the artist led a rugged life documenting and painting studies of birds. In 1826, he sailed to England with his collection *Birds of America.* His paintings were an immediate success, and he was given free painting lessons by the portrait artist Thomas Sully, who encouraged his efforts. In 1843, Audubon made his last trip west to create his final series of paintings, *Viviparous Quadrupeds of North America,* a study of mammals.

About the Artwork

Each life-sized, highly embellished bird portrait was depicted in great detail and accompanied by Audubon's descriptions and observations of wildlife. He would spend weeks painting day and night on some of his compositions, painstakingly rendering each feather or nuance of form. In *Carolina*

Parakeet, Audubon displayed the now extinct bird in numerous postures and drew attention to its rapidly dwindling population. At the time, Carolina parakeets were hunted for their feathers and regarded as pests, and farmers would shoot them by the thousands. This print is considered one of Audubon's most exceptional pieces.

About the Media

Audubon drew and painted using a combination of watercolors, graphite, gouache, crayon, and pastel on selectively glazed paper. He also painted some of his compositions in oils.

About the Technique

Audubon began drawing in the fields and forests of his home merely for recreation and enjoyment. As his career progressed he went on numerous expeditions around the country, climbing mountains and trees, and fording swamps and rivers, to obtain views of his subjects. Audubon studied a bird in its natural habitat and sketched it many times before beginning a final print.

Cecilia Beaux

1855–1942

Cecilia Beaux (sə sēl′ yə bō) was born in Philadelphia, Pennsylvania. When she wasn't working, Beaux studied at the Pennsylvania Academy where she later taught. In 1887, one of Beaux's paintings was accepted into the Paris Salon. This inspired her to travel overseas to continue her studies. For a year and a half Beaux studied in Paris at the Academie Julian and Colarossi. Returning to Philadelphia in 1889, Beaux's reputation quickly spread, with commissions from clients in Philadelphia, Boston, New York, and Washington D.C. Throughout her lifetime Beaux won awards for her work and received praise from her peers.

▲ **Cecilia Beaux.** (American). *Self Portrait.* 1894.

Oil on canvas. National Academy of Design,
New York, USA / Bridgeman Art Library.

About Art History

America's portrait tradition derived from Great Britain's long history of portrait painting. Colonial era painters such as John Smibert and Robert Feke produced flat portraits that lacked three-dimensionality. In the eighteenth century, John Singleton Copley introduced a more realistic style of portraiture through his use of shading and tonal composition. Artists who followed him—such as Gilbert Stuart, who painted portraits of George Washington—continued to produce realistically modeled portraits. In the late nineteenth century, Americans began to embrace European art, particularly impressionism. At first, impressionism's loose forms shaped by quick brushstrokes of bright color were greeted in America with mixed feelings. American painters wanted to make accurate portraits. Nevertheless artists such as Beaux increasingly experimented with the new style, especially in background areas and drapery.

About the Artwork

At 16, Beaux began art training with a relative, Catherine A. Drinker, who was a painter of historical and biblical subjects. By the time she was 18, she began to earn income using her artistic ability by teaching art and creating portraits of children.

About the Media

Beaux painted most of her portraits in oils on canvas. Many artists who traveled or painted outside used oil paint because it came in a tube and could be easily transported.

About the Technique

Oil paint is rich in color and texture and can be used in a variety of ways. Beaux made quick, strong brushstrokes in some areas of her paintings.

▲ **Attributed to John Bell.** (American).
Figure of a Lion. c. 1850–1860.

••

Glazed red earthenware. $8 \times 8\frac{1}{2} \times 4\frac{1}{2}$ inches
(20.32 × 21.59 × 11.43 cm.).
American Folk Art Museum, New York, New York.

John Bell

John Bell (jän bel) was born in 1800 in Hagerstown, Pennsylvania. From a very young age he was fascinated with creating clay objects. As a young adult, Bell opened his own pottery studio in Waynesboro, Pennsylvania. He and his wife, Mary Elisabeth, had nine children and enjoyed a comfortable lifestyle, thanks to the successful sales of his pottery. Bell died in Waynesboro in 1880. His five sons all became ceramic artists. They followed in their father's artistic footsteps and continued the family's pottery business.

About Art History

Bell was an American folk artist. His works had a simple beauty, characteristic of the style of middle-American artwork of the nineteenth century, but his designs, materials, and subject matter were original. He used a potter's wheel to create vases, jugs, and dishes, but his sculptures were formed by hand. Today Bell's ceramics are regarded as classic masterpieces of American folk art.

About the Artwork

This earthenware figure was made to serve as a doorstop. Its heavy clay construction made it an ideal item for securing the weight of a door. The body of the lion was finished with a yellow-toned glaze and the mane, tail, and eyes were finished in brown. The lion's teeth were detailed in white. The figure stands in a square, straight-legged pose, teeth bared and tail arching over its back in a forward loop. The tail loop probably served as a handle by which the lion doorstop could be lifted and carried.

About the Media

This sculpture was made from clay and a mineral glaze. It is reported that Bell experimented with making his own glazes and mixtures of clay from locally available materials. He often wrote to his brother, Samuel Bell, also a potter, about his experiments and ideas for new materials with which to create stoneware and earthenware pottery.

About the Technique

This sculpture was hand-molded by Bell, and probably detailed with delicate hand tools. He created the flowing mane and tail in a very clever manner: Bell forced soft clay through a very coarse mesh of burlap material, creating many tiny strings of clay set close together. After removing the burlap, Bell carefully arranged the clay strings to look like the flowing hair of a real lion. After these and other details were added, the sculpture was dried, glazed, and fired in a kiln.

7

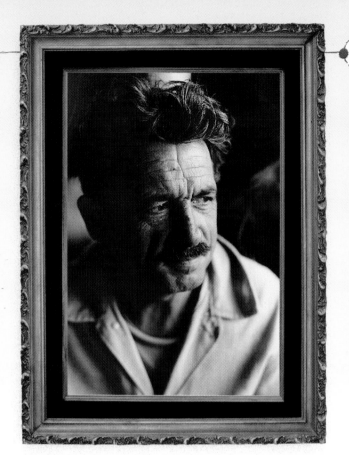

Thomas Hart Benton
1889–1975

Thomas Hart Benton (tom´ əs hart bent´ ən) was a regional American painter known for his energetic, colorful murals. He was the son of a United States congressional representative and named after his great uncle, a famous pre-American Civil War senator. From his family, Benton developed a strong identity as an American. He studied art in Paris and at the Art Institute of Chicago. Benton believed that American artists should develop their own styles and not just copy French painting styles. Although Benton began his art career as a cartoonist, he was known for his murals depicting scenes from the rural past of the American Midwest.

About Art History

Benton painted subjects from mostly one region —the American Midwest. He helped develop and promote the American art style known as *regionalism.* He urged American artists to paint scenes from the lives of ordinary Americans. He also encouraged his students to try new ideas in their work. One of his students was the famous painter Jackson Pollock.

About the Artwork

Benton enjoyed painting Midwestern farm scenes. Many of his paintings show sunburned farmers and huge work horses. In *Cradling Wheat,* several farmers and one of their sons are shown harvesting wheat by hand. Benton's paintings remind viewers of days gone by in rural America.

About the Media

Along with other media, Benton used oil and egg tempera.

About the Technique

Benton used his experience as a cartoonist in his later paintings by dividing scenes with borders, like a comic strip.

Paul Brach
b. 1924

Paul Brach (pôl bräk) was born and raised in New York City. Even though Brach grew up during the Great Depression, his family was not hit hard financially, and he was afforded a privileged education. As a teenager he spent his summers working on ranches in Arizona. He developed an appreciation for the freedom and space of the West, and evidence of this experience continues to appear in his paintings. He attended the University of Iowa, one of the first schools to offer a degree in creative work. After serving in World War II, Paul returned to the United States and married Miriam Shapiro, a widely respected painter whom he had met in Iowa. Today, Brach lives in New York and continues to ride his horse every Sunday.

About Art History

Paul Brach's earlier work is painted in an abstract expressionist style. *Abstraction* dealt with simple, orderly compositions. *Expressionism* was a manipulation of formal or representational elements to convey intense feelings. Abstract expressionism originated as an art movement in the early 1940s and included a variety of styles, not all of which were abstract or expressionistic. Surrealism and cubism had a direct effect on many abstract expressionists, and color field painting, gesturalism, assemblage and graffiti emerged from its influence. Some of Brach's contemporaries included Roy Lichtenstein, Bob Rauschenberg, Bob Irwin, Ed Kienholz and Larry Bell.

About the Artwork

In the 1980s, Brach became interested in the patterns he saw in the Navajo blankets of America's Southwest. He created several paintings in which he combined the patterns of the blankets with the monumental landscapes in which the weavers live. *Chuska* is the name of a mountain range in the northeastern corner of the Navajo reservation in Arizona. The blanket that inspired the pattern in Brach's work *Chuska* is in Santa Fe.

About the Media

Brach works primarily in oils on canvas. *Chuska* was created with oil and gold leaf on canvas.

George Catlin
1796–1872

▲ **George Catlin.** (American). *NO-HO-MUN-YA, One Who Gives No Attention.* 1844.
•••
Oil on canvas. 29 × 24 inches (73.66 × 60.96 cm.).
Smithsonian American Art Museum, Washington, D.C.

George Catlin (jorj kat´ lən) was born in Pennsylvania. He first became a lawyer, but painting lured him away from a law career. While painting miniatures in Philadelphia, he happened to meet a visiting group of Native Americans, and Catlin became fascinated by Native American culture. He made many trips into Native American territory and spent weeks studying groups that had not yet been influenced by European culture. He spent his own money to exhibit his paintings in England and France, where they were much admired. Living on a small income, Catlin traveled to South America to paint genre paintings of indigenous groups. Catlin has had more paintings displayed in the Louvre in Paris, France, than any other American artist.

About Art History

Catlin was the first artist to devote his entire career to painting genre paintings of Native Americans. His paintings are considered the most complete record of native groups in North and South America between 1830 and 1860. He insisted that no one could accurately paint these groups without living among them. Today, many Native Americans rely on his images for information about costumes and traditions of the past.

About the Artwork

Catlin eschewed stereotypical representations of Native Americans and created portraits showing their individuality. Examples include *Man Who Tracks* and *Red Jacket.* Catlin also painted Native American ceremonies, such as *Sioux Dog Feast,* and landscapes, such as *Buffaloes in the Salt Meadows.* Catlin created more than 500 paintings and wrote several books about Native American customs and ceremonies. He tried to sell his paintings to the United States government, but was unsuccessful.

About the Media

Catlin worked in both watercolors and oils.

About the Technique

Catlin thought of himself as a wilderness painter, not a studio painter. He often made quick, outdoor graphite or watercolor sketches before painting in oils in his studio. Catlin tried to depict his subject matter in the most realistic and accurate fashion possible.

▲ **Paul Cézanne.** (French). *Self Portrait with Hat.*
c. 1879
· ·
Oil on canvas. $44\frac{1}{2} \times 33$ inches (113 × 84 cm.)
Kunstmuseum, Bern, Switzerland.

Paul Cézanne
1839–1906

Paul Cézanne (paul sā zan´) was born in
the south of France in Aix-en-Provence.
He is often called the father of modern art.
He loved to paint, but people did not like
his work much—at least not during his
lifetime. He had to beg gallery owners to
show his work, and therefore he did not
sell many paintings. He inherited money
from his parents to pay his bills and buy
his paints. He continued painting until
a week before he died.

About Art History

Cézanne was a postimpressionist. He was greatly
influenced by the painter Camille Pissarro. Pissarro
introduced Cézanne to the new impressionist
technique for capturing outdoor light. Cézanne
combined impressionism with a formal instruction
the impressionists had abandoned. He looked
closely at things to find their basic forms and
shapes. Cézanne painted cylinders, spheres, and
cones to show these forms. Sometimes he changed
the shapes he saw in nature to make his paintings
more interesting. Picasso, Matisse, and other artists
studied Cézanne's ideas.

About the Artwork

Cézanne painted landscapes, still lifes, and
portraits. Many of his landscapes were of the
countryside and mountains near his home. He
developed a unique way of representing nature and
objects in a highly creative and abstract fashion.
Cézanne painted slowly, often taking several days
to create a still life. One friend posed 115 times so
Cézanne could finish his portrait.

About the Media

Cézanne worked in both oils and watercolors.

About the Technique

Cézanne used bright colors and bold brushstrokes,
especially in the skies of his landscapes. He applied
the paint in vertical and horizontal lines. He knew
that cool colors seem to pull back and warm colors
seem to go forward. Cézanne also used different
shades of the same color to add shape to his
subjects. His knowledge made his paintings seem
three-dimensional.

Chryssa
b. 1933

Born and educated in Greece, Chryssa (kris´ ə) first studied social work but redirected her career path, because she felt that many relief funds ignored people in need. She studied in Athens, Paris, and California, and began her artistic career as a sculptor in New York during the 1950s. Her exploration of neon light and commercial signs was a new combination of materials to the art scene and opened up many avenues for her public installations. Chryssa does her own metalwork and the physical labor required by her art. She is regarded as highly motivating by her coworkers.

About Art History

Chryssa's assemblage sculptures and concentration on form are a reaction against the widespread abstract expressionism of the 1950s. Instead of focusing purpose, she emphasizes the actual materials and signs of her artwork, drawing attention to their shapes and functions. In her earlier work she used pop images and letters of the alphabet, which set the stage for other pop artists, such as Jasper Johns and Andy Warhol.

About the Artwork

In her earlier work, Chryssa's sculptures featured commercial signs and lettering and were inspired by the teeming energy of New York's Times Square. Her first major work, *Times Square Sky,* was a turning point for her, as it was her first use of neon light. In many of her pieces, Chryssa relies on the reflective surfaces of metal to reverberate the glowing neon light as shown in her piece *Americanoom.*

About the Media

Stainless steel, welded steel, aluminum, neon, Plexiglas, signs, and flashing lights all come into play in Chryssa's artwork. Sometimes the lettering and lights are interwoven to create a bombarding force of visual stimuli that can be both overpowering and intriguing at the same time. This barrage of information is intended to evoke a wide range of emotion from her viewers—from fear to joy—just as one might feel if suddenly surrounded by an overflow of noise and bright lights.

About the Technique

Much of Chryssa's work incorporates welded steel and aluminum, which she manipulates and finishes herself, although some of her pieces use glass obtained from glassblowers or foundries. One of her major creations uses a timer that turns the neon lights on and off, and all of her sculptures require precise measurements and an understanding of electrical connections to be successful.

Helen Cordero

b. 1916

Helen Cordero (hel´ ən kôr dēa´ rō) began working with clay when she was 45 years old. After her children were grown, she was looking for a way to make a little extra money. When she began her craft, her bowls and jars kept coming out crooked. She was ready to quit when a friend suggested that she try making figures instead. She started to make frogs, birds, and eventually small figures of people. The first time she showed her figures, a folk art collector bought all her pieces and commissioned her to do a 250-piece nativity scene. Thinking of her *Singing Mother* piece, he also asked her to make a larger seated figure with children. Cordero said she thought about her grandfather who was always surrounded by children as he told stories. Remembering her grandfather's voice, she shaped her first *Storyteller Doll* in 1963, beginning a new Conchiti tradition.

About Art History

Cordero revived a nearly eradicated tradition of figurative pottery. When she shaped the first *Storyteller Doll* in 1964, she revived the Cochiti tradition of figurative pottery. Today, hundreds of potters are producing storyteller dolls. Some are animals, such as a storyteller bear covered with little cubs, and an owl singing to owlets.

About the Artwork

Cordero's *Storyteller Dolls* are usually seated with their eyes closed and their mouths open, as if they are singing or telling stories. Each of her figures is different. She never makes an exact duplicate.

About the Media

Cordero makes her figures from the red clay that is gathered on or near the reservation. She covers them with several coats of white slip. Then, red and black details are added. The black paint, or *guaco*, is made by boiling wild spinach (Rocky Mountain bee plant) into a sludge. This sludge hardens into a cake that is used like watercolor paint.

About the Technique

Cordero shapes each figure and lets it dry. Then she sands it smooth and coats it with a thin wash of gray clay and water. Cordero fires her figures on a grate in her yard. She applies more wash and fires the figures again until she achieves the color she wants. Finally, she paints on the faces, hair, and costumes.

Edgar Degas
1834–1917

Edgar Degas (ed´ gär dā gä´) was born in Paris, France, to a wealthy family. He studied law for a short time before discovering his interest in painting. Degas studied briefly at the École des Beaux-Arts in Paris around 1855. He worked at an artist's studio and traveled widely to study art. His early work showed a concern with classical painting, in subject matter as well as composition. His themes always dealt with people and city life, especially dancers at the theater. After 1909, Degas turned to sculpture due to failing eyesight. He left many wax models of dancers and horses that were cast in bronze after his death.

▲ **Edgar Degas.** (French). *Self Portrait.*

Sterling and Francine Clark Art Institute, Williamstown, Massachusetts.

About Art History

Degas joined the impressionist group and exhibited with them, even though he detested the name and never painted in a purely impressionistic style. He admired Italian Renaissance painters, such as Leonardo da Vinci. He also admired the French neoclassical painter Ingres, whose figures had the grace of Greek statues. In his own work Degas combined impressionism with the painting style of the Renaissance.

About the Artwork

Degas is famous for his portraits, especially those of ballet dancers. Unlike other impressionists, he enjoyed painting genre scenes of modern life. His painting of customers in a hat shop, for example, was unusual. At that time artists did not usually paint such ordinary places.

About the Media

Degas created oil paintings, pastel drawings, ink drawings, and bronze sculptures. He also produced a great number of lithographs, engravings, and monotypes.

About the Technique

Many impressionists painted outdoors and quickly. Degas chose to work slowly in his studio. He planned his pictures and completed sketches before he painted. He sometimes took paintings back after they had been sold so he could improve them. He applied paint sketchily to make his work look unplanned.

Degas wanted his subjects to look as if they did not know they were being painted. He cut figures off at the edges of the canvas to make his composition seem spontaneous and not posed. He also wanted viewers to feel as if they were part of the picture. For this reason, Degas included large, open spaces to welcome viewers into his paintings.

Robert Delaunay
1885-1941

Robert Delaunay (rō bar dā län nā) was born in Paris, France in 1885. After completing secondary school, he became an apprentice in a theatre set studio and began painting in 1903. He exhibited his realistic paintings a year later at the 1904 Salon d'Automme and continued to exhibit at the Salon des Independants until World War I, when he served in the military. He was fascinated with the interaction of colors and eventually developed his own abstract style.

◀ **Robert Delaunay.** (French). *Simultaneous Contrasts: Sun and Moon.* 1913 (dated 1912).

Oil on canvas. 53 inches (134.5 cm.) diameter.
The Museum of Modern Art, New York, New York.

About Art History

Between 1905 and 1907, Delaunay became friends with Henri Rousseau and Jean Metzinger and studied the color theories of Michel-Eugène Chevreul. His early neo-impressionist work was influenced by the artist Paul Cézanne, but slowly moved toward cubism by 1910. In 1911, Wassily Kandinsky invited Delaunay to participate in the first Blue Rider exhibition, and in 1912, he had his first solo show. That same year he began his *Windows* series, which inspired the poet Guillaume Apollinaire to invent the term *Orphism* or *Orphic cubism* to describe Delaunay's work. During World War I, Delaunay lived in Spain and Portugal, but he returned to Paris in 1920 to experiment with painted figurative themes. By 1930, he abandoned representative work entirely and returned to complete abstraction with compositions of circular discs and color rhythms.

About the Artwork

The term *Orphism* referred to the ancient Greek musician, Orpheus. Delaunay's abstract work relied on a scale of color, as can be seen in his 1913

Simultaneous Contrasts: Sun and Moon. The dreamlike, abstract shapes merge into one another in areas of energetic motion and smooth gradation and symbolize a musical and earthly harmony. His circular canvas is a symbol of the universe, and the painting represents the movement and rhythm of the cosmos and rotation of day and night. Delaunay was inspired to paint this work after reading Michel-Eugène Chevreul's treatise *On the Law of the Simultaneous Contrast of Colors.*

About the Media

Paris was often the inspiration for Delaunay's oil paintings. City streets, cathedrals, crowds and the Eiffel Tower can be seen in many of his representational compositions.

About the Technique

Delaunay researched color theory and applied it to much of his work. He incorporated his interest in the meaning and science of color into his abstract paintings, and he often collaborated with his wife, painter Sonia Terk.

The Dentzel Company

The Dentzel Company was started by Gustav A. Dentzel, a woodcarver who immigrated to America from Europe and settled in Philadelphia in 1860. Gustav Dentzel had already begun his career carving carousel horses in his native Germany, where he had learned the trade from his father. After arriving in America soon after his twentieth birthday Dentzel opened a cabinet making shop. Within seven years' time he succeeded in shifting the focus of his business to building steam- and horse-powered carousels.

◀ **Dentzel Company, Philadelphia.** (American). *Carousel Rabbit.* 1915.

Paint on wood with glass. $57\frac{1}{4} \times 49 \times 12\frac{1}{2}$ (145.42 × 124.46 × 31.75 cm.). American Folk Art Museum, New York, New York.

About Art History

Taking their name from the equestrian tournaments enjoyed by royalty in eighteenth-century France and England, carousels became popular in America during the early 1900s. Although they were invented in Europe, the rotating carnival rides were redesigned and improved upon in the United States, becoming more grand and elaborate as their popularity increased. Some famous American carousel artists of this period include Charles Looff of Coney Island, New York; two of Looff's apprentices, Marcus Illions and Charles Carmel of Brooklyn, New York; and artists Solomon Stein and Harry Goldstein, also of Brooklyn, New York.

About the Artwork

The more spectacular carousels were painted in festive colors, were adorned with bright lights and mirrors, and had musical accompaniment such as a pipe organ or piano. Dentzel carousels were unique because they featured a menagerie of carved horses and other animals.

About the Media

Dentzel Company carousel animals were carved from wood. The animals were painted with realistic detail and were sometimes given real horsehair tails.

About the Technique

William Dentzel was a third-generation woodcarver. Despite the passage of many years between the founding of the Dentzel Company in 1870 until its sale in 1928, the style and techniques used to create the wonderful carousel animals were preserved. The horses were modeled after real animals; every detail of their bodies, manes and tails, and facial expressions were carefully carved and painted by hand.

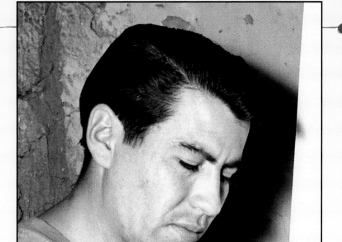

Patrick Des Jarlait
1921–1973

Patrick Des Jarlait (pa´trik dā zhär lā´) was born at Red Lake Indian Reservation in Minnesota. Growing up, he learned the traditions of the Chippewa, also called *Anishinabe* and *Ojibwe.* From the age of five, Des Jarlait loved to paint, sketch, and draw. He studied art in high school and at Arizona State, then served in the U.S. Navy during World War II. When he returned home, he continued to paint. He frequently gave talks to students about his Native American heritage.

About Art History

Des Jarlait belonged to the Red Lake Chippewa. He painted images of their traditions and customs to help preserve their way of life. Des Jarlait did not become famous while he was alive, but today many people consider his paintings important to the development of midwestern Native American art.

About the Artwork

Des Jarlait's paintings are stunning because of their bold shapes and bright colors. The faces of the people in his paintings are usually angular. He often painted Native Americans dancing, preparing food, or caring for children. Many of his paintings tell detailed stories about the Chippewa way of life and reflect their respect for the land.

About the Media

This artist usually painted with watercolors.

About the Technique

Des Jarlait made his people look crisp by using sharp lines for their noses, cheekbones, and jaws. He used mostly black and white to portray eyes, which created strong contrast. He painted clothes with bright colors, such as pink, yellow, and orange.

Richard Diebenkorn

1922–1993

Richard Diebenkorn (ri´ chərd dē´ bən korn) was born in Portland, Oregon, to a middle-class family. When he was two years old he and his family moved to San Francisco where he grew up drawing and painting, planning to someday be an artist. Diebenkorn's father did not support his artistic talents and ridiculed him for wanting to be a painter. Only his grandmother understood and encouraged him. When Diebenkorn was in college his father hoped his son would study business, but the young artist had his own plans and continued to paint. This determination and individuality paved the way for Diebenkorn's long, prolific career as an abstract painter and one of contemporary art's leading expressionist artists.

About Art History

Diebenkorn attended the University of Stanford, where he pursued the study of art and was influenced by the artwork of Edward Hopper, Paul Cézanne, Henri Matisse, Joan Miró, Baziotes, and Robert Motherwell. When he was drafted into the military and reassigned to the University of California at Berkeley, he encountered a school of thought based on the teachings of abstract painter Hans Hofmann and began experimenting with analytical painting methods. After World War II he taught at the California School of Fine Arts, where he was influenced by the work of Mark Rothko and Clyfford Still.

About the Artwork

In 1967 Diebenkorn accepted a professorship in painting at the University of California at Los Angeles and moved with his family to the beach. This change of environment inspired one of his most famous series of work, the *Ocean Park* series. These abstract paintings were large, contemplative, and referenced color field painting in their geometric lines and bold washes of color. Many of these works, such as *Ocean Park 105,* incorporate bright planes of pigment covering many layers of underpaint and thin straight bands of color. Some of the underpaint would drip and leak beyond the crisp borders of overpaint, causing the edges of original color to emerge, which added further intrigue to the compositions.

About the Media

The majority of Diebenkorn's paintings were completed with oil paints on large canvases. He composed a number of watercolor portraits while in the military, but none of these paintings survive.

About the Technique

Brosen painted the *Ocean Park* series with wide brushstrokes of paint that were sometimes thin and wash-like, and at other times thick and textured. In order to achieve the washed, layered appearance of his paintings Diebenkorn rubbed away areas of thin overpainting to let the colors beneath emerge.

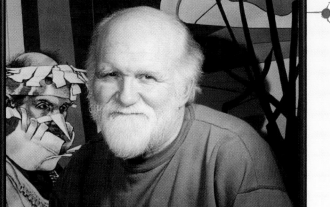

Ivan Eyre
b. 1935

Ivan Eyre (ī´ vən ēr) was born in rural Saskatchewan, a province in Canada. His family was extremely poor. They moved from place to place throughout Canada as his father looked for work. When Eyre was in fifth grade, he won a prize for painting. His teachers encouraged him to continue making art. He went to after-school art classes while he was in high school. After he graduated, he went to art school in Winnipeg. In 1967, the Canada Council paid for him to travel around Europe. He returned from his travels to teach in Winnipeg, Manitoba. He has also taught art at the University of North Dakota and the University of Manitoba.

About Art History

Ivan Eyre is an individualist in the art world. He does not belong to or work with any groups of artists. Eyre's work is difficult to categorize, because he often crosses boundaries of styles, themes, and media.

About the Artwork

In his artwork, Eyre tries to show how poverty and misery can be overcome with happy situations. Although Eyre has lived through wars, car accidents, and natural disasters, he wants to show that he has experienced more than this pain and anxiety. Most of his paintings combine elements of nature with those of civilization. Distorted figures that are long, angular, and unrealistically flat appear in many of his paintings. He paints many landscapes of wooded forests. Some of these appear to be seen through frames, as if the viewer is looking out a window. Sharp protrusions poke out of the frame toward the viewer.

About the Media

Eyre paints with acrylics and oils on canvas.

About the Technique

Eyre paints strong, heavy lines around his figures, which seem to float on his canvases. He uses analogous colors, usually all from one color family. The landscapes he paints show wide angles, often from above. His still lifes are set at unusual angles. They are often framed by a windowsill or an imaginary, unusually shaped frame. Sometimes Eyre applies shiny glazes over parts of his acrylic paintings to accent those areas.

Jacob Gay

Jacob Gay (jā´ kəb gā) was a professional engraver living in the Great Lakes region of North America during the mid-eighteenth century. It is believed that Gay engraved this powder horn in New York in 1759.

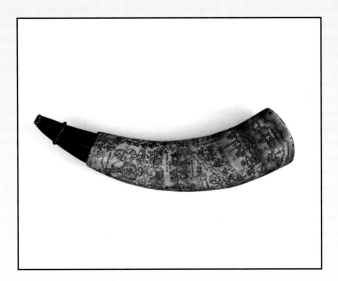

▲ **Jacob Gay.** (American).
Engraved Powderhorn. 1759.

Cowhorn. The Metropolitan Museum of Art. New York, New York.

About Art History

At the time this powder horn was made, the American territories were still British colonies fighting for their independence. This powder horn was carried by a British soldier, as is indicated by the engraving of the British coat of arms on its surface. Although the British and Americans considered one another enemies during the American Revolutionary War, not all British soldiers were willing to fight the colonists. Some young British soldiers were forced into service, and many were unhappy to be stationed in cold and foreign colonies far from their homes. Many deserted their military ranks and went into hiding, others married American women and even joined the colonists in their fight for independence.

About the Artwork

This powder horn was made as a container for carrying gunpowder. Powder horns were usually made from the hollowed out horns of large animals such as cows. A strap was sometimes attached to the ends of the powder horn, allowing a soldier to sling the strap over his shoulder. The end of a powder horn was usually equipped with a metal nozzle that made dispensing the powder and filling the rifle quick and easy. The powder horn shown here was painstakingly engraved with a map of the region where its owner was stationed.

About the Media

This powder horn is made of a cow horn and metal.

About the Technique

Gay used sharp hand tools to engrave a map of the Hudson Valley and the locations of forts from Albany, New York, to the Great Lakes. Also engraved into the surface of the horn are the name of its owner, Jotham Bemus, and the British coat of arms.

Adolph Gottlieb

1903–1974

The painter Adolph Gottlieb (ā´ dolf gät´ lēb) is perhaps best known as an early and outstanding member of the New York School of Abstract Expressionists. Gottlieb, a self-assured native New Yorker, studied at the Art Students League of New York before he ventured to France to study art at the age of 18. He traveled through France, Austria, and Germany before he returned to New York to attend Parsons School of Design, Cooper Union, and the Educational Alliance Art School. Due to health concerns, Gottlieb and his wife lived in Arizona from 1937 to 1938. When he returned to New York, he taught at the Pratt Institute in Brooklyn, New York.

About Art History

As an abstract expressionist, Gottlieb tried to show emotions in art through nontraditional means. He was influenced by the contemporary psychologists Freud and Jung and by the works of primitive, cubist, and surrealist artists. Gottlieb painted in two distinct styles: pictographs and "bursts." During his travels in France and Europe, he developed an appreciation of thirteenth- and fourteenth-century polyptychs, which influenced his pictograph style. The burst approach was developed after Gottlieb spent time in Arizona, where the unique character of the desert inspired him to paint landscapes with radically flattened spaces.

About the Artwork

Gottlieb's series of pictographs contain gridded compartments filled with symbols based on fantasy and the unconscious. Included in his pictograph paintings are images of body parts such as eyes, hands, and heads, as well as birds, fish, dots, and arrows. Gottlieb's *Burst* paintings are partial abstractions of landscapes that contain large, exploding orbs of color, reminiscent of solar bodies.

About the Media

Gottlieb painted with oil and tempera paints.

About the Technique

This artist used layers of oil and tempera paints to create contrasting surfaces. He painted most frequently on canvas, but occasionally on burlap. For his *Burst* paintings, he used larger canvases and usually painted in a three-hue palette (red and black against white).

Duane Hanson
1925–1996

Duane Hanson (dwān han´ sən) carved little figures out of logs using kitchen knives as a boy in his native Minnesota. Later he attended art school and taught art in Atlanta, Georgia and Miami, Florida. The same art dealer who discovered Andy Warhol arranged for Hanson's first solo exhibition. His life-size sculptures of ordinary people were an immediate success with the public. People could identify with his work. Hanson married and had five children. He continued to plan and create sculpture until the end of his life.

About Art History

Hanson's super-realistic style is so successful that people try to start conversations with his sculptures. One time a museum visitor dialed 911 to get help for an "unconscious" Hanson sculpture.

About the Artwork

Hanson created more than 100 sculptures during his career. His subjects were real people, ranging from janitors to sunbathers to athletes. One example is *Tourists,* a life-size and lifelike man and woman dressed in clashing clothing. Hanson's aim was to make viewers more aware of themselves and others. In a lighthearted way he tried to warn viewers not to want so much that they can never be happy.

About the Media

Hanson used a combination of polyester resin and fiberglass to create his sculptures.

About the Technique

Hanson often took six weeks or more to construct a sculpture. He began by choosing a model, often one of his friends. He posed the person and covered the model's body with petroleum jelly to keep the mold from sticking to the skin. He formed the mold by applying plaster bandages to parts of the model until he had made a mold of the model's whole body. After each mold dried and hardened, he removed it. Then he filled the plaster mold with a flesh-colored mixture of polyester resin and fiberglass to form the sculpture. After reassembling the parts, he painted the figure. Finally he added glass eyes, clothing, a wig, and accessories.

Auguste Herbin
1882–1960

Auguste Herbin (ō gūst´ âr´ ban) was born in France and studied at the École des Beaux-Arts. Later he went to other countries to paint. In Italy, he noticed how different kinds of light changed the way things look. From then on he tried to ignore little details and paint only the main part of his subject. Herbin was enthusiastic and curious and loved his work. During the last years of his life Herbin created tapestry designs.

About Art History

Herbin explored the geometric, cubist style of painting. He made the subjects in his paintings more and more simplistic until they were only outlines or symbols. He was interested in shapes and colors, and studied how different colors make people feel. Herbin also read about optical illusions and used them in some of his paintings. Herbin was a leader of the abstract creation school of art along with Georges Vantongerloo. Abstract creationists wanted to create purely abstract art, reducing their works to the basic elements of color and form. Wassily Kandinsky was another member of this school of painters.

About the Artwork

Early in his career, Herbin painted large still lifes and landscapes. In time his paintings became so symbolic that it was hard to tell what he had painted. His later paintings consisted of geometric shapes rendered in bright colors.

About the Media

Herbin most frequently painted with oils.

About the Technique

Herbin used flat, intense colors and bold shapes. Brushstrokes cannot be detected in Herbin's paintings.

David Hockney
b. 1937

David Hockney (dā′ vəd häk′ nē) was born in 1937 into a working class family in the northern industrial section of Bradford, England. By the time he was 11, he had decided to become an artist. At 16, he attended the Bradford School of Art, and went on to study at the Royal College of Art. In 1961, he made his first trip to the United States. The brightness and light of California was a sharp contrast from the rain and fog of England. He was impressed by the sense of space in the sprawling city of Los Angeles, and moved permanently to the United States in 1978 to become part of the California art scene.

About Art History

Hockney first made an impact on the art world in the 1960s. He was a leader of the English pop art movement that was centered in London, England. Pop artists were fascinated by how the flood of American mass media was affecting British life. Pop artists used popular or commercial culture as inspiration for their art.

About the Artwork

Hockney is a realistic painter who uses many styles and techniques to tell stories. Much of his artwork relates to his life, family, and friends. Hockney is inspired by the climate and culture of southern California. He is interested in the sunny blue skies and the relaxed lifestyle.

About the Media

Hockney paints with oils and acrylics. He is a stage designer, a printmaker, and a photographer. Hockney creates photo collages that he calls "joiner" photographs. He joins separate photos together to create a unique image that expresses time and movement.

About the Technique

Hockney paints with large areas of bold color. As his style developed he became more interested in how people view his work. He wanted to extend the gaze of his viewers. To create his "joiner" photo collages he alters and combines images to show the passage of time. He may repeat the same image or change the scale or the angle to imply movement. Hockney uses forward and backward progression and organizes all the images to guide the eye to a focal point. He uses an ordinary, automatic 35mm camera and takes a number of pictures in rapid succession.

Edward Hopper
1882-1967

Edward Hopper (ed´ wərd hä´ pər) was born in Nyack, New York. He attended the New York School of Art and made three trips to Europe to study art. He worked as an illustrator in New York City and eventually opened a studio in Greenwich Village. Hopper married another painter, Josephine Nivison, who helped arrange his first exhibition. They spent their summers on an island off the Maine coast, on Cape Cod, and at other East Coast locations. These spots became the settings of many of Hopper's paintings.

▲ **Edward Hopper.** (American). *Self-Portrait.* 1903.

Charcoal on paper. $18\frac{1}{2} \times 12$ inches (47 × 30.5 cm.).
National Portrait Gallery, Smithsonian Institution, Washington, D.C.

About Art History

Hopper was one of the finest realistic painters of his time. Although his style was realistic, he often adjusted reality to suit the image he had in mind. For example, he changed the size or shape of objects to create a better balance, or left out the trees or a street near a house he was painting.

About the Artwork

Hopper's works emphasize the loneliness of modern life. Although he lived in a crowded city, his scenes were usually empty of people. He preferred subjects that included water, such as lighthouses, rivers, and bridges. Another favorite subject was a large, old house, often surrounded by dead trees. Hopper occasionally added one or more people to such scenes.

About the Media

Hopper painted primarily with oils. He also made many watercolor paintings. His drawings were all studies that he used for his paintings. Hopper used charcoal, pencil, pen and ink, and conté crayon to create his drawings.

About the Technique

Early in his career Hopper often worked in the back seat of his car, which served as his studio on wheels. He began by outlining a scene with a pale pencil. Then he painted without planning, focusing on the structure and the light in the scene. In one painting, for example, he used a delicate, musty light to indicate early morning on a beach. In his famous painting *Nighthawks* a bright light that creates hard-edged shadows reveals a group of sad people at a lunch counter late at night. Hopper usually painted his watercolors outdoors.

Yvonne Jacquette

b. 1934

Yvonne Jacquette (e´ von ja´ ket) was born in Pittsburgh, Pennsylvania. She studied at the Rhode Island School of Design, and then moved to New York City. Her first exhibition was held in 1965. Jacquette has taught art in colleges and art schools. She is married to filmmaker Rudy Burckhardt and has designed sets for his movies. Jacquette and her husband often vacation in Maine; many of her paintings portray Maine landscapes.

About Art History

Jacquette was one of the leading painters of American New Realism during the late 1960s. At that time abstract and pop art were in style. Painting in a realistic style at that time was risky, but Jacquette believed that the lines between realism and abstract art were blurry. Therefore, her art blends the real and the abstract.

About the Artwork

Jacquette paints landscapes and cityscapes from an overhead point of view, as they would appear from a plane. She sometimes includes plane wings in her paintings and titled one painting *The Right Wing II.* Her subjects range from farmland landscapes to industrial sites.

Jacquette often paints night scenes. She shifts the dots and dashes of light in her paintings to form patterns. Some of her paintings show the conflict between people and nature. The subject of disaster is often a theme in Jacquette's painting. For example, she has painted the Three Mile Island nuclear power plant, which overheated and released radioactive gas in 1979. She has also illustrated books.

About the Media

Jacquette paints in oils and pastels and creates prints and frescoes.

About the Technique

Jacquette often works while looking out a penthouse window or the window of a small, circling plane. When she flies in airplanes she quickly sketches during takeoffs and landings. Sometimes she takes photographs during a flight. She uses them to jog her memory when she returns to her studio.

William H. Johnson
1901–1970

William Johnson (wil´ yəm jän[t]´ sən) was born in Florence, South Carolina. When he was young, a teacher saw him drawing in the dirt with a stick. She gave him pencils and encouraged him to draw more pictures. At age 17, Johnson went to New York to study art. While there he won many prizes. A teacher collected money so that Johnson could go to Paris, France, in 1926 to study art.

In the late 1930s, Johnson and his wife returned to the United States to escape the beginning of World War II. For a time he worked as a teacher, and in the early 1940s, he worked for the Works Progress Administration (WPA). The WPA was a government agency that gave jobs to people who were unemployed during the Great Depression.

▲ **William H. Johnson.** (American).
Self-Portrait. 1921.

Oil on canvas. $23\frac{1}{4} \times 18\frac{1}{4}$ inches (59.06 × 46.35 cm.).
Smithsonian American Art Museum, Washington, D.C.

About Art History

Johnson was part of the Harlem Renaissance of the 1920s. During this period African American artists, writers, musicians, and scholars flocked to Harlem in New York City. African American art, literature, and music thrived. Johnson painted scenes of African American life in an expressionist style. His later work looked like primitive art because of its simple, flat shapes. Johnson was a major American painter. His work has been exhibited in the National Museum of American Art in Washington, D.C., and in many university galleries around the country.

About the Artwork

Religious life, war, and farm life are themes found in Johnson's work. His paintings show great energy and have strong, bold lines. Johnson often painted serious subjects in a humorous way.

About the Media

Johnson worked in oils, watercolors, gouache, pen and ink, brush and ink, and pencil on paper, cardboard, or burlap.

About the Technique

Johnson used strong lines and simple shapes to express energy and movement.

Wassily Kandinsky
1866-1944

Wassily Kandinsky (va sēl´ ē kan din´ skē) first tried painting as a teenager in his native Russia. Even then he felt that each color had a mysterious life of its own. He was still drawn to colors and painting while he studied law and economics in college, but he believed that art was "a luxury forbidden to a Russian." In time, he moved to Germany, studied art, and began his career. Throughout his life Kandinsky moved back and forth between Russia and Germany. In 1933 he settled in France after Nazi storm troopers labeled his painting style "degenerate."

About Art History

Kandinsky was a pioneer in the pure abstract painting style—a combination of color and form with no subject matter. He did not give a title to a painting he did in 1910, but others called it the *First Abstract Watercolour.* Kandinsky felt that trying to paint recognizable objects distracted artists from their real jobs of expressing ideas and emotions. He believed communicating through painting was similar to communicating with music. He often gave his paintings titles that were musical and abstract, such as *Improvisation 30.*

About the Artwork

It is possible to identify landscapes and objects in some of Kandinsky's early paintings, but his later work was entirely abstract. Only occasionally during World War I did Kandinsky include cannons and other recognizable objects in his work.

About the Media

Kandinsky worked in oils, watercolors, and India ink.

About the Technique

Kandinsky did not try to show the essence of his subjects because he had none. Instead, he attempted to make forms and colors take on meaning separate from the physical world. His work often impresses even viewers who are not certain what the paintings mean.

John Frederick Kensett
1816–1872

John Frederick Kensett (jän fre´ drik ken´ sət) was born in Cheshire, Connecticut, in 1816. His father was an immigrant engraver, and Kensett first learned how to draw by working in his father's firm. As he spent more and more time with other artists, Kensett was persuaded to teach himself to paint, and this self-education led to further schooling in Europe. The mountainous regions of the American northeast were some of Kensett's favorite landscapes to paint, and he spent the later part of his artistic career painting landscapes of the Long Island Sound in his native Connecticut.

About Art History

Kensett painted in the Hudson River salon style as well as the protoimpressionist mode, and he admired Thomas Cole and Asher B. Durand, two of the leading landscape artists of the 1800s. A large number of Kensett's works were landscapes in the category of *luminism,* a style focused on an ultra-realistic perception of nature. A few of Kensett's luminist contemporaries were Martin Johnson Heade, Sanford Gifford, and Fitz Hugh Lane. Many luminist paintings can be recognized by their seamless attention to translucent and reflected surfaces. Luminism was a mode of artistic expression that hid the brushstrokes and presence of the artist, rendering the painter anonymous, as described in the American poet Emerson's writing. This form of painting emphasized a poetic approach, rather than an analytic approach, to capturing light and atmosphere.

About the Artwork

It is difficult for a viewer to see any of Kensett's brushstrokes, even when his paintings are scrutinized at a close range. Kensett included great detail in his paintings, especially in the foreground. Often his detailed foregrounds incorporated every leaf on a tree and each pebble in the sand of a shoreline. Some of his more well-known pieces include *Coast Scene with Figures* and *A View of Mansfield Mountain,* both of which exemplify his mastery.

About the Media

Kensett painted on canvases of both small and large dimensions. He used oil paints with many layers of glaze and small brushes to add precise detail. The layering of glaze contributed to the mysterious absence of visible brushstrokes.

About the Technique

During the spring and summer Kensett traveled outdoors making oil sketches of landscapes which he would then use as models for his intricate paintings during the long winter months.

Paul Klee
1879–1940

Paul Klee (paul klā) was born into a musical Swiss family. His family hoped he also would become a musician. At age five his grandmother gave him his first box of pencils. He thought of himself as an artist from then on, but he continued to have an interest in music. Klee played his violin for an hour nearly every morning of his life. He married a pianist. As an adult Klee still drew in a childlike way. Klee believed that childlike drawings were the most creative and original. He was not trying to share his ideas through his work. He just wanted to explore his imagination. Klee could use either hand proficiently when painting.

About Art History

At first, art critics ignored Klee's work. Then they realized that his small, charming, playful pictures were filled with ideas and meaning. Different people find different meanings in Klee's pictures. For many people this adds to the value of his work.

About the Artwork

Klee studied nature and often began his paintings with an image from nature. Then he would let his imagination take over.

About the Media

Klee painted with watercolors and other materials on paper, canvas, silk, linen, and burlap. He liked to experiment; for example, he did one picture with black paste on burlap.

About the Technique

Color was important to Klee. He once said, "Color and I are one; I am a painter." In his watercolors Klee used thin layers of pale color. This technique made his pictures gently shimmer like pavement under a hot sun. Klee used color the way a musician uses sound. He tried to touch the feelings of his viewers. Klee said that he learned more about painting from the musicians Bach and Mozart than he did from other visual artists.

Franz Kline
1910–1962

Franz Kline (fräntz klīn), was born in Wilkes-Barre, Pennsylvania, and is considered one of the most prominent twentieth century American abstract artists. He began his career as a landscape painter, and studied at the Art Department of Boston University and the Heatherly School of Art in London, England. During the early stages of his career Kline received awards in a number of National Academy of Design Annuals. After his schooling he lived in New York City, where he painted street and bohemian scenes until he began his exploration of abstract painting in 1946. When he enthusiastically committed himself to abstract expressionism in 1949, Kline was creating bold, large-scale works with great success. His vigorous style was unique, and at times his artwork was said to resemble urban landscapes.

About Art History

During the beginning of Kline's leap into abstract expressionism at the end of World War II, he was living in New York City. It was there that he became colleagues with Motherwell, Pollock, and other avant-garde artists, and they would hold open discussions about pioneering abstract expressionism. Kline focused on his own ideas and continued to seek an independent, dynamic approach to his artwork while working with the abstract expressionists.

About the Artwork

Abstract expressionists valued individuality and spontaneous improvisation. Each artist's style was unique, although all chose to move away from conventional subjects and styles. Kline was inspired to begin painting in the abstract expressionistic style when a friend put some of Klein's small sketches into a projector that magnified their strong linear quality and bold strokes. Much of Kline's early work reflects these projections, and are large, black calligraphic images on white backgrounds. At times his vigorous geometric lines echo the skeletons of buildings. It wasn't until the end of his career in the late 1950s that Kline began incorporating color into his linear abstractions.

About the Media

The intense gestural character of Kline's paintings is emphasized by size and visual movement. His canvases, some larger than six feet, were usually primed with a white background and then painted with black oil paint. Instead of canvas, Kline would at times use paperboard, which is easier to use and faster to prepare.

About the Technique

Before painting, Kline sketched his compositions, usually on the pages of a telephone book. When he was satisfied with an idea, he would use large house-paint brushes full of black paint on unstretched canvases attached to his studio walls. His powerful brushstrokes were applied with a lot of action and controlled consideration.

Jacob Lawrence
1917–2000

Jacob Lawrence (jā´ kəb lär´ ənz) had parents who met on their migration to the North. His father was born in South Carolina, and his mother in Virginia. Lawrence was born in Atlantic City, New Jersey, in 1917. The family finally settled in Harlem in 1929 at the end of the Harlem Renaissance. Because his mother worked all day, she enrolled Lawrence in the Harlem Art Workshop after school to keep him out of trouble. He had many excellent teachers there, including Charles Alston. Lawrence won a scholarship to the American Artists School. He taught at New York's Pratt Institute from 1958 to 1965. From 1970, he taught at the University of Washington in Seattle, where he also served as head of the art department. He won many awards in his lifetime, including the Presidential Medal of Arts.

About Art History

Lawrence's paintings not only contribute to the art world, they also add to our knowledge of African American history. Lawrence painted African American heroes, such as Harriet Tubman and Frederick Douglass.

About the Artwork

Lawrence's most famous work is a series of 60 paintings called *Migration of the Negro.* The paintings tell a story which begins at a train station in the South and ends at a station in the North. The scenes he chose to paint focus on the struggle of leaving one life for another and the search for freedom and dignity. His paintings did not overlook the harshness and violence that was part of this migration. During World War II he served in the

U.S. Coast Guard and created a series of paintings about his experiences. They were exhibited by the Museum of Modern Art in 1944.

About the Media

Lawrence painted on paper with *gouache,* an opaque watercolor paint, similar to tempera paint used in schools. It covers the paper with a smooth, matte coat. He was also a printmaker.

About the Technique

Lawrence said a lot about his subjects with only a few lines and carefully chosen colors. He used many neutral colors, such as taupe, mocha, and charcoal, and balanced them with splashes of bright color.

Leo Lionni
1910–1999

Leo Lionni (lē´ ō lē ō´ nē) was an illustrator, author, critic, art director, painter, sculptor, printmaker, cartoonist, and teacher. Born in the Netherlands, he grew up in an atmosphere of social and political revolution and came to appreciate art at a young age through his uncles' art collections. Without formal training in children's literature, Lionni began writing by chance. In 1959, he found himself responsible for entertaining his two grandchildren on a long and boring train ride. He tore blue and yellow shapes from the pages of a magazine, made his briefcase into a stage, and improvised a story about the two colors. The result was his first book, *Little Blue and Little Yellow,* which was soon followed by other children's books and four Caldecott Honor Books.

About Art History

Futurism and the modernist tendencies of Bauhaus art influenced Lionni's architectural terrariums and designs, though his earliest art education came from numerous childhood trips to local museums where he would sketch great works of art. When he was a young man he moved his family to Milan, the Italian center for avant-garde artists, and began writing about European architecture for a local magazine. Lionni eventually branched into advertising design in the 1930s. By 1939, Italy was becoming a stronghold for fascism, and Leo was pressured to declare whether or not he was Aryan. He decided to immigrate with his family to the United States and settled in Philadelphia, Pennsylvania, where he became a successful art director for the Ford Motors advertising company. In 1948, he moved to New York and became the art director for *Fortune* magazine. Twelve years later he returned to Italy. Lionni began his career in children's books when he was 50 years old.

About the Artwork

In addition to dreamlike colors and organic forms, Lionni's books incorporate themes such as race relations, the value of art, and political issues. His characters face individual and social challenges. The book *Swimmy* is about a little black fish who helps a school of frightened red fish work together to swim bravely through the ocean. Teamwork and individuality are important in this story.

About the Media

The bright illustrations in *Swimmy* and Lionni's other books are created with watercolors, torn paper, and textured crayon collages.

About the Technique

Lionni often gained ideas for his books and illustrations from sudden bursts of inspiration, such as his dreams, though the majority of his works were shaped through hard, disciplined work. He created many drafts and sketches of a story before reaching the final version.

Robert Lostutter

b. 1939

Robert Lostutter (räb´ ərt lō stut´ ər) was born in Kansas. He attended the School of the Art Institute of Chicago, and has been a participant in many exhibitions. His work has won three Logan Prizes and a Tuthill Prize, among others. Lostutter has made many trips to Mexico, and the influence of Mexican culture and geography can be seen in his work.

About Art History

Regional art is created by artists who were born in or who are very interested in a particular area. Regional art was once only realistic, not abstract. Artists in Chicago, Illinois, and Houston, Texas, have helped make imagist art popular. *Imagist art* is regional and abstract. Lostutter is known as a Chicago imagist. The works of the Chicago imagists combine abstract images and realism.

About the Artwork

Most of Lostutter's work shows figures that might be acrobats. They are usually held by hands or ropes. Their skin and costumes seem tight, as if they were sewn on. The figures seem to hold each other back and support each other at the same time. Some of Lostutter's figures have birdlike heads or masks. Others have flowers on their chests or heads. The activity in these paintings is unclear, partly because Lostutter shows only part of the figure. For example, a figure's head might be outside the painting's borders. The meaning of the painting is up to the viewer to decide. Lostutter also paints prehistoric leaves and fish.

About the Media

This artist paints in watercolors and oils on canvas.

About the Technique

Lostutter spends a great deal of time preparing sketches and watercolors before he begins to paint. He often adds glazes or enamels to his work, and then repaints in order to get the surface texture he wants. Light plays an important part in Lostutter's paintings, giving his figures a strange beauty.

René Magritte
1898-1967

René Magritte (rə nē´ mə grēt´) was born in Belgium at the end of the nineteenth century. After studying art in Brussels, he worked briefly in a wallpaper factory. The influence of his time at this factory is sometimes evident in his patterned paintings. Magritte had a mischievous attitude, and displayed an avant-garde, poetic energy. He directed this energy into numerous creations and was honored with retrospective exhibitions in both Europe and the United States.

About Art History

Surrealists valued fantastic, absurd and poetic images. They also valued the artwork of children or the untrained amateur artist because they were thought to create from pure impulse and to be free from convention. Although Magritte did not paint in a childish hand, he was a contemporary of fellow surrealist artists Joan Miró, André Breton, Jean Arp, Salvador Dalí, and Paul Eluard. In both group and solo exhibits Magritte's work was shown in galleries in Brussels, Paris, New York, and London, and is represented in many museums.

About the Artwork

The poetic nature of language interested Magritte, and he admired the way it combined with a visual image to make viewers question the context and intent of his paintings. *La Vie des Aire (The Voice of Space)* seems to ask these questions. Its floating spheres and landscape contradict reason and tell a story that cannot be easily read. Magritte didn't abandon realism in his paintings but transferred realistic objects, such as a tree, chair, or clock, into a dreamlike environment or behavior. In *The Fall*

he painted men wearing overcoats and bowler hats falling from the sky onto a town below. Pattern and a muted palette make their way into a number of Magritte's works as well as some of his commissioned murals in Brussels.

About the Media

Magritte worked with oil paints on canvas.

About the Technique

Magritte employed free association in the philosophical interpretation of his paintings. He would make sketches of his subjects and then use light brushstrokes on his canvases to create a dreamlike airiness.

William McCloskey

1859–1941

Realist painter William McCloskey
(wil´ yəm mə kläs´ kē) was born in
Philadelphia, Pennsylvania, where he
studied at the Pennsylvania Academy of
Fine Art. He was married to the artist
Alberta Binford, who was also a highly
regarded realist painter. The two of them
set up a portrait studio together and
traveled widely across the United States
and Europe, earning acclaim for their
acutely realistic paintings.

About Art History

While he was at the Academy, McCloskey was
influenced by Christian Schussele, who emphasized
the importance of studying still life subjects. This
influence remained strong throughout McCloskey's
career as he traveled from city to city, holding open
houses with his wife and establishing themselves in
the art community. Los Angeles, New York, London,
and Paris were cities the McCloskeys frequented,
and they exhibited with acclaim almost everywhere
they went. It was not unusual for William and
Alberta to work on a painting together.

About the Artwork

McCloskey is best known for his series of still-life
paintings of oranges wrapped in paper. The orange
series included many works with a horizontal
format, triangular composition, reflective tabletop,
and lush dark backdrop. McCloskey also produced a
number of *genre paintings,* which are depictions of
people involved in everyday activities. A majority of
his portraits were of his daughter, Eleanor, and
were watercolors. Most pre-Civil War painters
focused on portraying the nostalgia and innocence
of childhood, which was different from the earlier

representations of children as burdensome or
as laborers.

About the Media

In addition to small oil paintings of still lifes and
portraits, McCloskey and his wife created
a number of paintings of famous actors and
actresses dressed in elaborate costumes.

About the Technique

McCloskey set up his still lifes in the studio and
created sketches and final compositions directly
from his arrangements. McCloskey also painted
portraits by referencing his posed subjects, but
there have been photographs found of his daughter
that are similar to some of his paintings, which
indicate that he may have used photo references
as well. He achieved immense detail and realism
by observing his paintings through a magnifying
glass, then touching up the composition with
minuscule drops of paint.

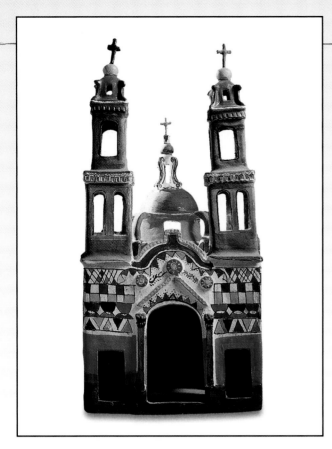

▲ **Herón Martínez Mendoza.** (Mexican).
Church. c. 1960.
....
Painted earthenware. 24 inches (60.96 cm.) high.
Museum of International Folk Art, Santa Fe, New Mexico.

Herón Martínez Mendoza

1918–1989

Herón Martínez Mendoza (ā ron´
mär tē´ nez men dō´ zə) was born in Mexico.
Like his parents, grandparents, and great-
grandparents, he began his career by
creating cooking pots. He had played with
clay since childhood, but he did not want
to become a potter. To support himself
and his wife, he began making clay barrels,
which sold well. Growing up, Mendoza
listened to many myths and legends. These
stories—and his own creativity—inspired
him to create unique and beautiful pottery
reflecting the myths and legends of his
childhood. In his later years, he stayed busy
filling orders for sculptures requested by
individuals and museums. Mendoza and
his wife had six children.

About Art History

Mendoza, a self-taught artist, became one of
Mexico's most extraordinary folk potters. He based
some of his designs on bits of ancient pots found
near his village; other designs were based on
his imagination.

About the Artwork

Perhaps Mendoza's best known pieces are his clay
candelabras. Each begins with a central figure that
supports the rest of the structure. The candleholders
grow upward and outward on graceful wings. He
often created pieces in animal forms that represent
the fantasies and legends of his childhood.

About the Media

Mendoza worked in clay, which he sometimes
finished with polishes of different colors.

About the Technique

Mendoza depended on his imagination for most of
his designs. He also gained inspiration from
religious or spiritual sources in his life.

Maria Sibylla Merian
1647–1717

Maria Sibylla Merian (mä rē´ ə si´ bil ə mer´ ē ən) grew up in a house full of artists. Her father was an artist and publisher. Her stepfather was a still-life painter, engraver, and art dealer. Merian was surrounded by a large collection of prints, paintings, and books and benefited from her stepfather's artistic instruction. Merian published a number of books on flowers and on the metamorphoses and eating habits of caterpillars. An independent woman, Merian traveled with her daughter to Suriname in South America, where they lived for two years.

About Art History

The seventeenth century witnessed an explosion of scientific inquiry in the Netherlands. The greatest trade nation at the time, its influence and culture spread around the world. Merchants and travelers to other countries brought back animal, insect, and plant specimens, which Dutch collectors eagerly purchased. Merian's interest in visiting Suriname was sparked by seeing those specimens. Her studies revolutionized zoology and botany.

About the Artwork

Her insect and plant studies brought Merian renown. She was sought after for her paintings and scientific knowledge. Although her engravings look like still lifes, they were actually illustrations for important scientific volumes about the preferred foods and life cycles of insects.

About the Media

Merian sketched and painted on vellum, which is calfskin that has been treated for use as a writing surface. She may have executed a few engravings herself, but studio engravers probably created most of the copper plates used for printing her work.

About the Technique

Engraving has been practiced since the fifteenth century. Artists have experimented with the process, sometimes leaving ink on the plate to give the print's background a slight color instead of keeping it all white. Engraving was an inexpensive way to reproduce many copies of a painting for book illustration.

Louise Moillon
1610–1696

Louise Moillon (lü ēz´ mwä lôn´) was one of the earliest French artists to specialize in still-life painting. Her father was a painter and picture dealer, and most likely her teacher. By the time she was 11, her artistic talent was evident. Most of her dated work was produced between 1629 and 1641. She married in 1640 and had three children. Later in her life she again produced paintings with dates, perhaps because of financial need. As a Calvinist, she and her family suffered persecution after the 1685 repeal of the Edict of Nantes, which granted religious freedom to Protestants in France.

▲ **Louise Moillon.** (French). *Still Life with Cherries, Strawberries and Gooseberries.* 1630.

Oil on Panel. $12\frac{5}{8} \times 19\frac{1}{8}$ inches (30.07 × 48.58 cm.). Norton Simon Museum, Pasadena, California

About Art History

During the seventeenth century, especially in northern Europe, *still lifes,* arrangements of natural objects such as fruits and flowers, and human-made objects, gained importance. Moillon specialized in still lifes of fruit, but sometimes included figures in her compositions. She and other French artists are credited with creating a distinctive school of French still-life painting. Restrained compositions with subtle color harmonies and precise descriptions of objects are typical of Moillon's style.

About the Artwork

Moillon's careful technique produced naturalistic images of fruit. Often an arrangement of fruit was placed in the center of the composition and balanced by other fruit placed beside it on a ledge.

About the Media

Moillon painted with oil on canvas. Oil paints are created by mixing dry pigments with oil.

About the Technique

Pointed leaves and jagged branches add variety and contrast to the smooth, round contours of the fruit in Moillon's still lifes.

Claude Monet
1840–1926

Claude Monet (klōd mō nā´) did not want to be a painter as a young man in France. He was already well paid for drawing caricatures of tourists. Painter Eugene Boudin saw talent in Monet's exaggerated drawings and encouraged him to paint. Although artists were "supposed" to paint in studios, Boudin urged Monet to paint outside in the open air. There Monet learned to capture his first impressions on canvas. He recorded these impressions during a long and productive life. His greatest wish was to "mingle more closely with nature."

About Art History

Monet made a large contribution to the development of impressionism through his ideas and paintings. Unlike most painters before him, Monet painted outdoors. He made careful observations of subject matter, studying the changes in appearance due to light and weather. In the first impressionist exhibition, Monet included a work titled *Impression: Sunrise.* A critic, ridiculing the colors, strange distortion of shapes, and loose brushstrokes, derived the name *impressionism* from this title. The term *impressionism* was soon accepted and used by the public to describe this new style of painting.

About the Artwork

Monet painted landscapes and people but especially loved scenes that included water. At one time he had a floating studio. He filled a rowboat with art supplies and painted in the shade of a striped awning. Toward the end of his life, Monet painted huge landscapes of the garden and lily ponds near his home in Giverny, France.

About the Media

Although he made sketches later in life, Monet created mostly oil paintings. By the 1870s, Monet eliminated black from his palette, replacing it with blue.

About the Technique

Monet often began a painting by covering the canvas with a background color. Then, he dabbed paint here and there until shapes became recognizable. He was fascinated by the way the same color could look different at certain times of the day or during particular weather conditions. He often painted the same subjects over and over again to capture this in his paintings. Examples of motifs he painted include Rouen Cathedral, poplars, haystacks, and water lilies.

Henry Moore
1898–1986

Henry Moore (hen´ rē mor) was born in Castleford, England. When he was ten, he told his father he wanted to become a sculptor. At 18, he left home to join the army during World War I. He began studying art after the war. By age 23, he was a serious sculptor.

About Art History

In the 1930s, many sculptors were producing realistic works. However, Moore and a few of his artist friends started creating sculpture that was more abstract. Moore simplified human figures and emphasized carving forms. He used holes in his sculptures, which he associated with the mystery of caves. His early works show the influence of Mexican and African carvings. Many critics consider Moore the greatest English sculptor of the 1900s.

About the Artwork

Moore frequently combined his figures with shapes and textures from nature. He focused on making the simplest form of the subject he carved. Moore thought of his large sculptures as part of the open air with the sky as the background. Families were an important subject of his sculptures. His own family inspired his work.

About the Media

Moore carved some sculptures in wood and some in stone. Most of his large sculptures were cast in bronze.

About the Technique

Moore collected pebbles, flint rocks, shells, animal bones, and old, weathered pieces of wood for his studio. These pieces inspired him to draw. From his sketches, he made small models for his sculptures, then he made larger models. After much planning he was ready to make the actual sculptures.

Jesús Moroles
b. 1950

Born in Texas to Mexican immigrant parents, Jesús Moroles (hā sōōs´ mo rō´ lēz) creates monumental sculptures from granite, or "living stone." He has been working with granite since 1980 and now has his own successful studio headquarters—Moroles, Inc.—in Rockport, Texas. Moroles's sculptures have been exhibited all over the world, and he has had great success from the very beginning of his career. Often more than 20 feet tall, his massive creations can be found in numerous museums, as well as in outdoor environments such as the CBS Plaza in New York City, the White House sculpture gardens, the Edwin A. Ulrich Museum in Kansas, and the Albuquerque Museum in New Mexico. In 1996, Moroles opened the Cerrillos Cultural Center (C3), an exhibition, performance, and studio space in Cerrillos, New Mexico.

About Art History

After working in Italy for a year, Moroles returned to Texas in 1980 to apprentice with sculptor Luiz Jiménez. Moroles's giant granite sculptures began earning recognition right away in his early exhibitions. In 1982, Moroles received the Awards in the Visual Arts Fellowship which established his work in a two-year traveling exhibition. Word of his talent spread, and he began making large sculptures and fountains for commissions around the country. In 1985, he received a National Endowment for the Arts Matching Grant for a 45-piece installation of sculptures and fountains in the Birmingham Botanical Gardens of Alabama. He has earned national acclaim for his artwork and continues to lecture about his work and the issue of public sculpture.

About the Artwork

Moroles's granite sculptures weave together ideas of age-old history and contemporary America. In *Georgia Stele* he evokes concepts of Earth, his

Mexican American heritage, and Mayan culture by using ancient granite from Georgia in a modernized form. His sculptures can be very big; *Lapstrake,* a granite work that stands 22 feet high, weighs 64 tons, and the Houston Police Officers Memorial covers 14,400 square feet.

About the Media

When he first began creating sculptures, Moroles was told to use fiberglass that looked like stone instead of actual granite. He did not take this advice, however, because he believes that a strong spiritual connection exists between an artist and stone. The granite he uses comes from varied locations, and he works on it in his Texas studio.

About the Technique

Moroles hammers five-inch steel wedges into large slabs of granite, which cause them to split. Some of his surfaces are polished, and others are left unfinished.

Grandma Moses
1860–1961

Anna Mary Robertson Moses (an´ a mâr´ ē ro´ bərt sən mō´ zəz) was always interested in art but was too busy raising children and doing farm work to devote much time to her creative talents. It was not until she was in her late 70s that she took up painting. In 1938 her work was discovered when an art collector saw one of her paintings hanging in a drugstore window. Within two years her work was being exhibited at the Museum of Modern Art and the Galerie St. Etienne, both in New York City. In the last 20 years of her life, her paintings appeared in museums and galleries throughout the United States and Europe. She continued to paint until the year she died at age 101.

About Art History

Grandma Moses is regarded as a *folk,* or *naïve,* painter because she never had any formal training. She had to invent her own techniques to depict her subject matter. Even though some critics did not take her seriously, her paintings were popular and were reproduced on posters, fabrics, plates, and greeting cards.

About the Artwork

Landscapes were among Moses's favorite and most frequently painted subjects. Her paintings do not follow the conventions of perspective but rather rely on scale and color to create an illusion of depth.

About the Media

Moses preferred board to canvas because it made a painting more durable. Pressed wood is a type of fiberboard often used for insulation or paneling.

She applied paint in thin, opaque colors. It is likely that Moses chose to work with oils because of their versatile color range, durability, and the fact that the color does not change as it dries.

About the Technique

Moses began her paintings by treating a board with one coat of linseed oil. She then applied three coats of flat white house paint to the board to create a neutral ground. Over this she sketched rough details with a pencil. From her lifelong work with embroidery and textiles, Moses learned how to break things down into separate sections of color. The effects of this method caused some critics to compare her work to an impressionistic style.

Louise Nevelson
1900-1988

Louise Nevelson (lōo ēz´ ne´ vəl sən), one of the most important and successful American sculptors of the twentieth century, was born in Kiev, Russia. Her family resettled in Rockland, Maine, when she was five years old. As a child she began assembling wood scraps from her father's contracting business. Her education was rich and varied, including music, theatre, dance, and visual art. She studied in New York, New York and Paris, France. At first she made both paintings and sculptures, but eventually concentrated on sculpture, which she exhibited irregularly from the 1930s onward. It was not until the late 1950s that she began to receive critical acclaim. Before her death, she had received more public commissions than any other living sculptor.

About Art History

During the twentieth century the art of Africa, Oceania, and pre-Columbian America was studied. Artists also began to take interest in the visual and mythic powers these cultural artifacts possessed. Louise Nevelson was influenced by tribal and Mayan art. Her work has a modern, totemic power that links contemporary art styles to ancient civilizations.

About the Artwork

By painting her sculptures all black, white, or gold, Nevelson transformed the typical meanings of her found elements. These elements are combined to express both formal and thematic concerns. Toward the end of her career she worked with more abstract, geometric shapes. Many of her large public sculptures are made from steel.

About the Media

Nevelson used found wooden objects to create many of her works.

About the Technique

The paint on Nevelson's sculptures unifies the many shapes, but allows the grain of the wood to show through, giving liveliness to the abstract forms.

Taqialuk Nuna
b. 1958

Taqialuk Nuna (tah kē´ ə lūk nōōnə) was born and raised in Cape Dorset, a rapidly growing Inuit community located on the southwest coast of Baffin Island in the Canadian territory of Nunavut. The son of Inuit artist Sharky Nuna, Nuna is a self-taught carver and a member of the West Baffin Eskimo Cooperative. Nuna works in an outdoor studio even when the temperature drops to the negative forties. His serpentine sculptures reflect the natural life of his arctic environment and portray a respect for the power, beauty, and intelligence of other living creatures. He also uses his art to express the sense of fear, awe, and mystery people have about the forces that shape our lives.

About Art History

Without formal artistic training or studies, Nuna taught himself to carve by observing his family and community members at work. A diverse range of sizes and stylization exists in Inuit art, as some artists employ a representational approach to their creations and others are influenced by abstraction. Common themes of Inuit art include arctic wildlife, depictions of Inuit men, women and families in traditional dress and activities, and transformation pieces that represent imaginative creatures from the Inuit shamanistic tradition.

About the Artwork

In addition to being an independently taught and successful artist, Nuna is also a very good hunter. His hunting skills are self-taught and adapted to his specific area, and they provide him with further inspiration and understanding of the animals he carves. This experience with hunting factors into his art and helps him portray the behaviors of his subjects in addition to their appearances.

About the Media

Polar bears and human figures are often the subjects of Nuna's carvings as are beautiful masks made from stone used solely for decoration. He has worked with marble, alabaster, and granite, although he predominantly uses serpentine, a marbled green rock native to northern Canada and the Cape Dorset area. Nuna is presently working with smaller sculptures and will sometimes travel great distances to acquire his preferred stone.

About the Technique

Instead of traditionally sketching or planning his carvings on paper, Nuna observes the stone from all sides, peering into it and intuitively envisioning the finished sculpture without a model. He then uses chisels, handmade tools, prospector's tools, grinders, and drill bits to allow his design to emerge.

Georgia O'Keeffe

1887–1986

Georgia O'Keeffe (jôr´ jə ō kēf´) was born in Sun Prairie, Wisconsin. At the age of ten she began taking private art lessons, but the thing she liked most was experimenting with art at home. By 13, she had decided to become an artist. She trained under experts and won many prizes for her art. For years she challenged the art world with her unique vision. She eventually became famous for her spectacular, larger-than-life paintings of natural objects, including flowers, animal skulls, and shells. She loved nature, especially the desert of New Mexico, where she spent the last half of her life. O'Keeffe was married to the famous American photographer Alfred Stieglitz and appears in many of his photographs. In 1997, a Georgia O'Keeffe Museum opened in Santa Fe, New Mexico. It is the first museum in the United States devoted exclusively to the work of a major female artist.

About Art History

Stieglitz promoted modern artists and photographers from Europe and America through a magazine called *Camera Work* and a gallery known as "291." O'Keeffe and the circle of artists she met through Stieglitz were pioneers of modernism in the United States. She took subjects into her imagination and altered and simplified their appearances. She expressed her emotions through her vivid paintings.

About the Artwork

O'Keeffe's artwork features bold, colorful, abstract patterns and shapes. She most often painted natural forms such as flowers and bleached bones, pulling them out of their usual environments. She never painted portraits but sometimes painted landscapes.

About the Media

O'Keeffe used oils and watercolors for her paintings. She used pastels, charcoal, and pencil for her drawings.

About the Technique

O'Keeffe worked in dazzling, jewel-toned colors. She chose unusual perspectives, such as very close up or far away. She also enlarged the scale of her subjects.

James Peale
1749–1831

James Peale (jāmz pēl) was born in Chestertown, Maryland, in 1749. When he was 13, he worked in his brother's saddlery, and several years later he became an apprentice to a cabinetmaker. When his older brother Charles returned from London as a trained artist in 1769, Peale became his assistant and student and earned a reputation for his detailed, realistic paintings. Peale served during the American Revolution as a first lieutenant until 1779, and then resided in Philadelphia with Charles until 1782. His popularity as a romantic artist eventually grew and earned him a respectable following of patrons and collectors. His three daughters continued the "Peale Dynasty" and became successful still-life artists as well.

▲ **Charles Wilson Peale.** (American).
James Peale. 1822.

Oil on canvas. The Detroit Institute of Arts, Detroit, Michigan.

About Art History

During the eighteenth century, *romanticism* was an approach that focused on the subjective feelings of the artist. In the late 1700s, *romantic naturalism* became the predominant force behind landscape painting and revolved around the scientific or factual representation of nature. When Peale's eyesight began to fail in 1810, he discontinued creating miniatures and turned to large landscapes and still lifes.

About the Artwork

While Peale was serving in the American Revolution, he painted two full-length portraits of George Washington at Yorktown. Peale's subjective approach depicts Washington in a brave, commanding stance. His elongated limbs and direct gaze imply Washington's masterful persona, and the crisp appearance of Washington's surroundings and habit suggest that the war was for a triumphant and glamorous cause. This painting also served to gain public support for Washington's leadership.

About the Media

Miniatures, or small portraits, were a fashionable item in the eighteenth century. They were more affordable than large commissioned pieces, and their diminutive size meant that an artist could create great quantities of them in a short period of time. More people began to purchase portraits and small still-life paintings because of the miniatures' greater availability.

About the Technique

Peale sketched and painted his compositions using a model. A subject would pose for him while he made sketches and color studies and then return whenever Peale needed to study color, shape, or detail.

Rosalind Ragans

b. 1933

Rosalind Ragans (ro´ zə lind rā´ gənz) was born and grew up in New York City. When she was 11, polio paralyzed the right side of her body. Fortunately two years of therapy helped her regain nearly all the movement she had lost. Ragans had planned to be a stage designer but discovered that she loved teaching art. She began teaching in New Jersey in 1956. She earned a doctoral degree in education. While teaching art in Georgia in 1975, she began developing *ArtTalk*. This art education program presents art as a language, or way of communicating. Published in 1987, it has been well received by art teachers across the nation. Since then Ragans has created *Art Connections*, which you are using now. She still finds time to create the batik paintings she loves.

About Art History

Ragans works in a style of her own that approaches abstraction. Like two artists she admires, Alice Neel and Frida Kahlo, she uses her art to deal with personal conflicts. For example. Her *Self Portrait*, subtitled "My Soul Dances," expresses her mind's ability to dance even though her body cannot.

About the Artwork

All of Ragans's batik paintings have dancers and plants in them—either as the main subject or hidden in the background. Ragans has always loved music and dancing. She is also fascinated by plants because she saw so few of them as a child in New York City.

About the Media

Ragans uses dyes and untreated rayon, cotton, linen, and silk to create her batiks.

About the Technique

After sketching an image on fabric, Ragans uses hot wax to cover the areas she wants to remain white. Then, she applies the colors, beginning with the palest ones. After each color dries, she covers it with hot wax so that it will not be affected by later colors. The last step is removing most of the wax with paper towels and an iron. Any remaining wax adds a glow to the image.

Pierre-Auguste Renoir

1841–1919

Pierre-Auguste Renoir (pyâr ō gōōst´ ren wär´) was one of the most widely known and best-loved European painters. The sixth of seven children, Renoir was born into a poor family in Limoges, France. His father was a tailor, and the family had to live in a slum, with few luxuries or comforts. Renoir showed signs of talent at an early age in many artistic fields. Although he was a talented singer, he became an apprentice at a porcelain factory, where for five years he copied French masterpieces onto plates and soup tureens. During this apprenticeship Renoir developed his brushwork and his passion for the eighteenth century French master painters such as Watteau and Boucher. Renoir's work became more widely known in the 1880s, after a decade of struggle and lack of recognition.

About Art History

Renoir was one of a group of artists known as the impressionists. These artists, including Monet, Pissaro, Sisley, and Morisot, followed the advice of the poet Baudelaire to abandon historical subjects and to show the beauty of modern life instead. In attempts to record truthful and direct responses to nature they painted outside rather than inside the studio. They painted quickly in order to capture the scenes in front of their eyes before they changed. The impressionists were known for their bold, rapid technique. They covered the surfaces of their canvases with broken touches or slashes of color. The impressionists began exhibiting in 1874, and were met with extreme criticism and public hostility. Many people were unable to understand their style. Today, exhibitions of impressionist artists are greeted with much excitement.

About the Artwork

Renoir studied art for two years at the famous École des Beaux-Arts in Paris, France. He learned to draw there, but he disregarded academic guidelines that did not allow him to develop his own personal style. He discovered a new style of painting not based on the feathery brush strokes of impressionism. During this period, he also began to concentrate on using women and children as his subject matter.

About the Media

Renoir most frequently used oils or pastels.

About the Technique

Renoir painted on a white background. For the first layer of color he used paint so diluted that it ran down the canvas. Then he would cover the surface of the canvas with tiny brushstrokes of pure color.

Simon Rodia
c. 1875–1965

Simon Rodia (sē´ mōn rō dē´ ä) was born in Avelino, Italy. He moved to the United States when he was 14 years old. He lived with his brother in Pittsburgh for a few years and then moved to California. He worked during the day as a tile setter for a construction company. Every evening, weekend, and holiday he built towers and sculptures in his yard in Los Angeles. He liked to read about heroes in history, such as Marco Polo, Christopher Columbus, and Galileo. Rodia once said that a person has to do "good good" or "bad bad" to be remembered. He worked for 33 years to build his fantastic *Watts Towers*. By the age of 75, Rodia had grown tired of his neighbors laughing at him for making his art. He completed all the sculptures in his yard and then moved away from Los Angeles.

About Art History

Rodia was an *outsider artist*, a self-taught individual who works in isolation from the art world. These artists do not show their work in museums, galleries, or universities where mainstream art is displayed. Another outsider artist who made public sculpture was a Frenchman, Ferdinand Cheval.

About the Artwork

Rodia built three soaring towers, the *Ship of Marco Polo*, and a complex of arches, fountains, and pavilions in his yard in Los Angeles. The skeletal *Watts Towers* are almost 100 feet tall.

About the Media

Rodia collected more than 70,000 seashells to create *Watts Towers*. He disassembled many pipe structures and steel bed frames. He salvaged truckloads of ceramic tiles and glass bottles from other people's trash. His towers are made of reinforced concrete, which consists of cement poured over steel rods. Rodia used over 7,000 bags of cement.

About the Technique

Rodia worked alone. He climbed his towers wearing a window washer's belt and a burlap pouch filled with shells, dishes, figurines, mirrors, and tiles. He carried a trowel and a pail of cement. He applied cement to the towers and then arranged pieces from his burlap sack into a decorative display on the wet cement.

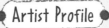

Miriam Schapiro
b. 1923

Miriam Schapiro (mir´ ē əm shə pir´ ō) is an American artist who was born in Toronto, Canada. She grew up in the Flatbush section of Brooklyn, New York. Her parents encouraged her pursuit of a career in art and sent her to art classes at the Museum of Modern Art. She met her husband, artist Paul Brach, while attending college. They married in 1946 and have a son who is a writer. Schapiro organizes her home life so that art is woven into it. She can move from baking in the kitchen to painting in her studio and back to the kitchen without feeling interrupted. Her husband says that she has learned to live a "seamless life."

About Art History

In the beginning of Schapiro's career, her work was abstract expressionistic. Later she became an important leader in the feminist art movement of the early 1970s. She wanted art to speak as a woman speaks. In art history, women's art has been hidden. Even the materials that women have used—lace, fabric, tea towels, ribbon, sequins, buttons, rickrack, yarn, silk, cotton, and so on—have been left out of art history.

About the Artwork

In time, Schapiro's work became more geometric and structured. In the 1950s, she expressed her identity by including feminist themes in her art. In 1972, Schapiro and other female artists changed an old Hollywood mansion into a totally female environment and called it "womanhouse." Schapiro and Sherry Brody made *The Dollhouse*—a construction of bits of fabric and tiny household objects meant to reflect female life and fantasy. Schapiro also made "femmages." She and a few other artists invented this word to describe art made with techniques that women traditionally use, such as sewing, embroidery, piecework, and appliqué. *Femmages* are collages that reflect female emotions and creativity.

About the Media

Schapiro uses fabric scraps, sequins, buttons, threads, rickrack, spangles, yarn, silk, taffeta, cotton, burlap, wool, and other materials a person might use in daily life.

About the Technique

Schapiro uses collage, assemblage, and decoupage to join materials.

Wilhelm Schimmel
1817–1890

Wilhelm Schimmel (wil´ helm shim´ məl) was born in Hesse-Darmstadt, Germany, and moved to the Cumberland Valley near Carlisle, Pennsylvania, just after the Civil War. He earned a living by carving birds and animals to sell or to trade for food and a place to sleep. At the time of his travels his carvings were not seen as successful works of art, but they are now regarded as some of America's finest folk art pieces and are sold at auctions for thousands of dollars. One characteristic of Schimmel's work is a lack of signature; he never signed his name on his carvings. Because he traded small carvings for meals, they were often set aside in attics or storage closets and were not discovered until nearly a century later.

About Art History

Little is known about Schimmel's life in Germany. When he arrived in the Cumberland Valley, he was around 50 years old and was not accompanied by any family member. His meager lifestyle in Pennsylvania prompted him to go from place to place, often working odd jobs and tramping around the countryside. Schimmel earned a reputation as a heavy drinker with a surly disposition, and his whimsical, untrained carvings could be found in saloons, barrooms, and fashionable rural homes within 30 miles of Carlisle.

About the Artwork

The most famous of Schimmel's works are his large, dramatic eagles painted in bright colors and spanning lengths from a few inches to a few feet. They have smooth bodies with crosshatching, and each feather on their wings and bodies stands out clearly. The eagles were usually decorated with a combination of black or brown and contrasting bright colors, such as green, red, or yellow.

About the Media

Schimmel carved almost exclusively in soft pine and used various paints to decorate his work. Soft pine is ideal for hand carving, but flat soft pine boards tend to warp in damp weather and over time. Schimmel traveled with few possessions, so his carved works were painted with whatever paint he could find.

About the Technique

Schimmel used basic tools and had no formal training. His nomadic lifestyle caused him to rely on few belongings, so he carved his sculptures with a small jackknife and pieces of glass, and he used only a few old brushes to paint them. He collected pine scraps from sawmills or carpentry shops and covered them in gesso or plaster before painting them. Sometimes, when supplies were available, Schimmel finished his carvings with varnish as a final aesthetic element.

John Scott
b. 1940

John Scott (jän skät) was born in New Orleans, Louisiana. He received his bachelor of fine arts degree from Xavier University there. After earning his master of fine arts degree from Michigan State University, Scott returned to New Orleans. He spends his time creating artwork, working in the community, and teaching art at Xavier University.

About Art History

Whether sculpting, painting, or making woodcuts and prints, Scott usually works in an abstract style. In the early 1980s he studied with George Rickey—a sculptor known for his movable structures that change the way space appears—and it had an important influence on his artwork. In his artwork, Scott explores the African American experience, the rich culture of New Orleans, and the musical styles of jazz and blues.

About the Artwork

John Scott often focuses on traditional African American musical instruments and the work of African American jazz artists in his sculptures and other artwork. Although he uses an abstract style, many of his works communicate social and spiritual messages. Scott believes "the thing that makes art is when you have form and content and you cannot distinguish between the two."

About the Media

Scott creates paintings, woodcuts, prints, and metal sculptures.

About the Technique

Many of John Scott's sculptures combine metallic materials with strong colors. His kinetic sculptures have hinged or hanging pieces that move with every breeze. This feeling of movement and energy spills over into his paintings and woodcuts.

Lorenzo Scott

b. 1934

Folk artist Lorenzo Scott (lor´ n zō skät) was born and raised in Georgia and began drawing when he was five years old. He has been a construction worker and house painter, yet he has also made a name for himself as a talented fine artist. In 1968 he traveled to New York and was so inspired by artists painting in the streets that he went home determined to do the same thing. Without any formal training, Scott taught himself to paint by studying oil paintings of the old masters in Atlanta museums.

▲ **Lorenzo Scott.** (American). *Ballet Dancers.* 2001.
....

Oil on canvas. 50 × 30 inches (127 × 76.2 cm).
Collection of Ann and Ted Oliver.

About Art History

Though he is a devout Baptist, Scott's work is full of traditional themes of New Testament Roman Catholicism. His biblical scenes depart from traditional Renaissance art by depicting Jesus and his disciples as African.

About the Artwork

Scott uses large canvases and bright colors, and his subjects seem to appear at the front of the composition without evidence of expansive depth. Though he was inspired by famous artists, Scott is not a copyist. He has created a unique style and is respected in folk-art circles across the United States. Scott's early contact with Renaissance painters filtered into his own subject matter. His oil paintings focus on biblical stories of the Old and New Testament, baptism, heaven, and the life of Jesus. Recently, his themes have grown to include secular imagery and country scenes.

About the Media

Scott works in oils on canvas.

About the Technique

Scott applies thin layers of oil paint on canvas or wood panel. He also builds his own frames, and his material is completely innovative. Scott uses an automobile body filler to sculpt the frames for his paintings. When the filler dries, he applies gold leaf, which mimics the appearance of the classical gold frames seen in museums.

James J. Shannon
1862–1923

Known as J. J., James Jebusa Shannon (jāmz sha´ nən) was born in New York to Irish parents. Even as a boy, he showed drawing talent, so he was sent to England in 1878 to study at the Royal College of Art. Several of his instructors at the college were French artists. A promising student, Shannon was asked to paint a portrait of a female staff member of the queen. This picture marked the beginning of his career as a portrait painter.

◄ **Orlando Rouland.** (American).
J. J. Shannon, R. A. c. 1910.
....

Oil on frabric canvas mounted on fiberboard.
$45\frac{1}{4} \times 34\frac{1}{4}$ inches (115.4 × 87 cm.).
Smithsonian American Art Museum, Washington, D. C.

About Art History

Artist James Whistler once insisted that Shannon resign his membership in the Royal Academy of Art because its artists had become "too commercial." Shannon made a good living painting portraits; he did not resign.

About the Artwork

Shannon painted portraits of the wealthy, of ordinary people, and of his own family. He wanted to create an image of beauty, not just a picture that looked like his subject.

About the Media

This artist painted with oils on canvas.

About the Technique

Shannon's work showed the influence of his French instructors, but his style varied from painting to painting. Some of this was due to his own experimentation, but at times he had to adjust his style to please the person he was painting. His work was sometimes light and impressionistic; at other times it was dark and realistic. Some of his best paintings were of his wife and daughter.

David Smith
1906–1965

David Smith (dā´ vəd smith) was born in Decatur, Indiana. He studied art during high school through a correspondence course with the Cleveland Art School in Cleveland, Ohio. He then attended Ohio University in Athens, Ohio, and the University of Notre Dame in South Bend, Indiana. In 1926, Smith studied at the Art Students League in New York. He taught art at many colleges, including Sarah Lawrence College in New York, and Bennington College in Vermont. Smith became interested in the welded-steel sculptures of Picasso while studying in New York. Drawing on skills learned while employed in a car factory one summer, he used his welding experience to construct welded-steel sculptures. He was the first American to do so.

About Art History

Smith is considered an abstract expressionist. This style of art seeks pure expression through form and color. He was one of the most important American sculptors of the twentieth century.

About the Artwork

Smith often incorporated machine parts into his early sculptures. In the 1940s and 1950s he began to create delicate sculptures inspired by landscapes. Gradually his sculptures grew larger and simpler, and by the 1960s he was crafting huge, geometric works. Much of his work is two-dimensional and is intended for view from one side.

About the Media

Smith is best known for creating sculptures out of welded steel, but he also made ink prints and oil paintings.

About the Technique

Rather than casting metal sculptures in molds, Smith constructed his sculptures out of sheets of metal and wires. Smith polished some of his most famous outdoor sculptures so they reflected the sky, the sun, and the colors of nature.

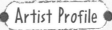

Edward Steichen
1879–1973

Edward Steichen (ed´ wərd stī´ kən) was born in Luxembourg and immigrated to the United States with his family when he was still a child. Steichen initially trained as a painter and took up photography to aid in making drawings for a lithographic firm. Steichen met the photographer Alfred Stieglitz while passing through New York on his way to Paris. Stieglitz not only purchased many of Steichen's photographs, he encouraged him to continue experimenting with the camera. During World War I, Steichen was chief of the photographic division of the Army Air Corps, and in World War II he directed a U.S. Navy combat photography team. Steichen is also known for his photographs of noteworthy personalities such as Auguste Rodin, Charlie Chaplin, and Greta Garbo.

About Art History

In 1902, Steichen joined Alfred Stieglitz in the founding of Photo-Secession, an organization dedicated to promoting photography as a fine art. In 1947, Steichen was appointed director of photography for the Museum of Modern Art in New York. In 1955, Steichen curated a photographic exhibit called "The Family of Man" for the Museum of Modern Art. The 503 photographs in the exhibit, compiled from amateur and professional photographers, focused on the real-life subject of human solidarity and became the most influential exhibition of photography at the time.

About the Artwork

Steichen initially gained popularity because his photos resembled paintings. During World War I, Steichen aimed for maximum realism. It was at this time that he began to develop photography as a modern art form that could capture everyday life.

About the Media

Steichen's medium was photographic film.

About the Technique

In Steichen's earlier work, he frequently brushed silver salts or other chemicals onto negatives or paper in order to achieve soft, fuzzy pictures. Sometimes he kicked his tripod to create a blurry image. These misty pictures were considered by most critics of his day to be the highest achievement of photographic art. As his career progressed, he tried to create photographs with maximum detail, definition, and brilliance.

Joseph Stella
1877-1946

Joseph Stella (jō´ sef ste´ lə) was born in Italy. He came to the United States as a young man and began painting portraits of immigrants living in New York City. A group that was concerned about immigrants was impressed with Stella's work. The group sent him to the coal mines and industrial regions of Pennsylvania and West Virginia. Stella painted the workers there so others would understand the terrible working conditions they faced. Stella saw how the growth of industry and the use of machines was affecting human lives. However, he was also impressed by the power and creativity of the American industrial age. In time, he turned from painting workers to painting symbolic pictures of technology and machines.

About Art History

Stella was one of the first artists to combine European abstract painting techniques with modern American subjects. Following the abstract style, Stella did not try to show realistic details. Instead, he represented what he saw with a combination of forms, colors, lines, and surfaces.

About the Artwork

Stella painted the Brooklyn Bridge several times because he felt its lines and angles represented the energy and opportunity of New York City. His paintings of the bridge have been used on posters and in textbooks and exhibitions to symbolize the city. In fact, people are so fascinated by these pictures that they tend to overlook Stella's later work. In his later life, he was influenced by his Italian background and more traditional painting styles. He created impressive landscapes, portraits, religious images, and still lifes.

About the Media

Stella most often created oil paintings.

About the Technique

Stella combined several points of view in the same picture. He used vivid, glowing colors and geometric patterns.

Roxanne Swentzell
b. 1962

Roxanne Swentzell (rokz´ an swent´ zəl) was born in Taos, New Mexico. She is half Native American. When she was a little girl she watched her mother make pots out of the clay surrounding their home. Swentzell liked to shape clay into figures. She had a hard time talking to other people, and tried to express her feelings through the figurines she made from clay. Her family saw that she was very talented. As a teenager she attended the Institute of American Indian Arts and the Portland Museum Art School. She went to college at the Pacific Northwest College of Art. She currently works and lives in Santa Clara, New Mexico.

About Art History

Swentzell's family includes five generations of potters, sculptors, architects, and teachers. There are many Native American artists who no longer make traditional Native American art, such as beadwork and pottery, because they are trying to break the stereotypic images of Native Americans. Swentzell and other artists make art that shows they are trying to balance a modern, mainstream life with a respect for the traditions of Native American culture.

About the Artwork

Swentzell makes large, hollow figurines that reflect Santa Clara Pueblo stories, her life, and the lives of those around her. She explores the emotions of people through her art. Swentzell communicates universal feelings through the body positions, hand gestures, and facial expressions of her figures. Many of Swentzell's sculptures are one color and void of decoration. Her figures are large, but restricted to the size of her kiln.

About the Media

Swentzell uses clay indigenous to her area of the United States to create her ceramic sculptures.

About the Technique

Swentzell uses a coil technique to make her sculptures. She forms a hollow body, then adds arms and legs. To make a face, she uses her fingers and knife to sculpt the clay, then she polishes the surface with her knife. She lets each sculpture dry for several weeks before firing it in a kiln.

Minerva Teichert
1888–1976

Minerva Teichert (mi nûr´ və tī´ kûrt) was born in Utah, the second of ten children, and grew up on a ranch in Idaho. She was encouraged by her parents to read and to appreciate music, literature, drama, and art. She considered herself an artist at the early age of four, when her mother gave her a box of watercolors. Teichert was fascinated with drawing and used her talent to tell the story of her Mormon community. Teichert painted images of western frontier life and interpretations of the scriptures, which are still used today in many Church of Jesus Christ of Latter-day Saints publications.

About Art History

Teichert graduated from high school at the age of 16 and began teaching school in Idaho to earn enough money to attend the School of the Art Institute of Chicago. When her father refused to let her travel to college alone she became a church missionary and traveled with a church group to Chicago. She became the first woman to be sent for art lessons with an official blessing of the Latter-day Saints church leadership. After graduating from college Teichert received a scholarship to attend the Art Students League in New York where she studied under Robert Henri and George Bridgeman, two famous realist painting instructors. Henri encouraged her talent and inspired her to return home and paint the history of the Mormon people.

About the Artwork

Many of Teichert's paintings are of pioneer and Native American subjects in the western wilderness. She often depicted human figures and work animals through a narrative, as in her famous painting *Night Raid*. In this painting, a thundering herd of horses and a Native American rider rush across the picture plane. The dynamic lighting of the night scene is emphasized by a bright white horse in the center of the pack that seems to illuminate the dark rocks nearby. Teichert's best-known works are her paintings of Mormon life and scriptural stories printed by church publications.

About the Media

Teichert painted with oils and created pencil and pen-and-ink sketches.

About the Technique

While Teichert was a student in New York, she developed a vigorous brushstroke technique similar to Robert Henri's. Her passion for painting remained strong throughout her life, and she drew on whatever surfaces were available at her home, including boards, flour sacks, aprons, walls, doors, the margins of books, and brown paper bags. She used neighbors and family members as models and referenced the animals and landscape of Utah in her compositions.

Tom Thomson
1877–1917

Tom Thomson (tom tom´ sən) was born in Claremont, Ontario, Canada, to a Scottish family. He was a quiet, modest man who lived a simple life. He began his art career by working as a commercial artist. He was very interested in Canada's Far North. At the age of 35, he decided to try to paint landscapes, so he quit his job. In only three and a half years, Thomson finished nearly 300 sketches and two dozen oil paintings. At first, not many people respected his artwork. Lumberjacks and trappers who knew the Far North were among the few who did. Thomson did not have much money. However, after his death, his paintings became popular. Now they hang in many Canadian galleries. Small sketches that he could not sell for 25 dollars have since sold for thousands of dollars.

About Art History

At a time when few Canadians were painting, Thomson was one of the Group of Seven. This Canadian group helped promote the country's artists, landscape, and people. Thomson helped other Canadian artists create their own styles. He let them know they did not need to copy European painting techniques. His style is known as *regionalism*. Thomson, an expert canoeist, drowned in 1917 in the lake he loved to paint. He was only 40. The shack where he lived and painted alone has been restored as a museum.

About the Artwork

Thomson mainly painted landscapes of the region of Algonquin Park in Ontario. He worked from early spring until the November snows, using oils to portray the wildlife, lumber camps, and landscape.

About the Media

Thomson worked mostly in oils on canvas.

About the Technique

Thomson's early work as a commercial artist helped him master the techniques of painting. He painted using rich, natural colors.

Harold Town

1924–1990

Harold Town (hâ rəld toun) was born in Toronto, Canada, and painted there almost all his life. He exhibited his work with a group of Canadian painters called the Group of Seven. He had his first one-person show when he was 30 years old. He created paintings and drawings in many styles.

About Art History

Town is usually called an *eclectic artist* because he painted in so many styles. Some of his paintings were inspired by the art of Native Americans and Vikings. Other works used imagery from Japanese or Chinese paintings.

About the Artwork

Some of Town's paintings look like big, colorful cartoons of muscular men. He also drew pictures of people with oddly shaped bodies. Other works are entirely abstract. He sometimes painted detailed and colorful patterns that make people want to touch his paintings.

About the Media

Town generally worked with oil paints on pressed wooden board or canvas. He also made collages, black-and-white prints, and ink drawings.

About the Technique

Many of Town's paintings incorporate decorated designs. He drew simple shapes, such as squares or triangles, all over a canvas and filled them with vivid colors, such as bright blue or hot pink. In his collages he used colored pieces of paper and often painted them. In his series of paintings of muscular men he drew the men's huge arms and legs with bold strokes of paint.

Leo Twiggs
b. 1934

Leo Twiggs (lē´ ō twigs) often draws from his experiences as a youth in South Carolina to produce his artwork. He has a doctorate of art from the University of Georgia and has won numerous awards and recognitions from organizations around the United States. Twiggs's accomplishments in teaching art to disadvantaged African American students earned him the title "Outstanding Young Man of America" in 1970. He is also the first visual artist to receive the Governor's Trophy for outstanding contribution to the arts in South Carolina.

About Art History

The early twentieth century began with a surge of African American themes in art created by African Americans. Often these works made social commentaries on the African American experience in America. Many times this imagery was compiled into an experimental artistic style based on Euroamerican art history.

About the Artwork

Twiggs began experimenting with the traditional batik process in 1965, and he eventually created his own personalized technique. Instead of having only flat, defined areas of color, Twiggs manipulates the wax and dyes to overlap in some areas.

About the Media

After he has completed the batik process, Twiggs works on cloth as if it were a canvas on an easel. He often applies pastels, colored pencils, and graphite.

About the Technique

To create a batik piece, the artist sketches a drawing onto fabric. Melted wax is applied to specific areas of the drawing with a utensil called a wax pen. The waxed areas retain the original color of the cloth throughout this process. After the wax cools, the cloth is dipped into a dye solution. The dye colors all parts of the cloth not covered with wax, and the cloth is left to dry. Before adding another color, the artist will use the wax pen over areas chosen to remain the previous dye color. The wax cools, and the cloth is dipped into a different dye solution and dried. The artist repeats this process again and again. Sometimes the wax cracks as it cools. This allows dye to enter an area the artist intended to remain the previous color. This seepage creates tiny dark lines in those areas. After the cloth has been dried for the last time, it is dipped in boiling water to melt and remove the wax.

Vincent van Gogh
1853–1890

Even as a boy in the Netherlands, Vincent van Gogh (vin´ sənt van gō´) cared about other people very much. He tried many jobs, including being a teacher, minister, and social worker. However, he had problems getting along with nearly everyone except his younger brother, Theo. At the age of 28, van Gogh decided that the best way he could serve others was through art. He expressed his deep feelings about people through his paintings. As he moved from place to place, he left many of his works behind. Some were burned in fireplaces for heat, and some were even used to patch holes in walls. Van Gogh was poor his entire life and often went hungry so that he could buy painting supplies. He died at age 37.

▲ **Vincent van Gogh.** (Dutch).
Self-Portrait with a Straw Hat. 1885.

Oil on canvas. $16 \times 12\frac{1}{2}$ inches (40.6 × 31.8 cm.).
The Metropolitan Museum of Art, New York, New York.

About Art History

Even though van Gogh sold only one painting in his lifetime, he is now considered the greatest nineteenth-century Dutch artist. He was one of the first to express his feelings through painting. This new school of art is now called *expressionism*.

About the Artwork

Van Gogh painted many different subjects, from portraits to landscapes. He once lived in France near fields of golden wheat and sunflowers, which he painted many times. He wrote that his sunflowers symbolized his gratitude toward others, especially his brother, who was one of the few people who encouraged him to paint.

About the Media

During the ten short years that van Gogh worked, he created hundreds of oil paintings, along with many drawings in ink, crayon, chalk, and charcoal.

About the Technique

Van Gogh wanted to show energy and motion in his work. He often put complementary colors, such as red and green, next to each other to add power to his paintings. He applied oil paints in thick layers, sometimes straight from the tubes. His thick layers, slashing brushstrokes, and swirling shapes give his paintings strong patterns that reflect his strong feelings.

Beatrice Whitney Van Ness
1888–1981

Beatrice Whitney Van Ness (bē´ ə tris hwit´ nē van nes´) was born and raised in the suburbs of Boston, Massachusetts. When she first began painting in art school she was regarded as a prodigy. Her work was so respected that the school hired her as a professor before she had even graduated. In addition to her own artwork, teaching was important to her, and she published a number of articles on art education.

About Art History

While studying at the School of the Museum of Fine Arts of Boston from 1905 to 1913, Van Ness was an avid student, learning from her American impressionist professors Edmund Tarbell, Frank Benson, and Philip Hale. In the mid-1920s she studied with the New England landscape painter Charles Woodbury, from whom she learned to depict the effects of bright sunlight. Between 1921 and 1949, Van Ness founded, directed, and taught in the art department at the Beaver Country Day School near Boston. She also taught at five other schools and participated in numerous international expositions. She continued to paint until the age of 91.

About the Artwork

Van Ness was commissioned to paint portraits, still lifes, and interiors, but she was best known for her brightly-colored outdoor scenes. The subjects of these compositions were often her own family and friends, and her summer vacation home in Maine provided inspiration for many of her paintings. *Summer Sunlight* was painted in one of these idyllic settings and depicts her family and a neighbor by the beach, illuminated by the warm summer sun. The dramatic sunlight surrounding the figures becomes the main subject of the painting, which the title indicates.

About the Media

Van Ness painted with oils on canvas. The luminous quality of oil paints allowed her to depict the warmth of sunlight in her compositions.

About the Technique

When Van Ness vacationed in Maine during the summers she made oil and watercolor sketches outdoors in the bright sunlight and shipped them back home to Massachusetts where she completed them. Her brushstrokes were broad and expressive.

▲ **Rembrandt van Rijn.** (Dutch). *Self-Portrait.* 1629.
....
Oil on panel. 35⅓ × 25 inches (89.7 × 73.5 cm.).
Isabella Stewart Gardner Museum, Boston, Massachusetts.

Rembrandt van Rijn
1606–1669

Rembrandt van Rijn (rem´ brandt vän rīn´) was the most influential Dutch artist of the seventeenth century. The seventh of nine children born to a miller and his wife, Rembrandt showed talent early in life. His parents took great interest in providing him with an education despite their modest income. Rembrandt studied a short time at the Leiden Latin School in the Netherlands to prepare for a profession as a city administrator. His parents eventually removed him from school and placed him in apprenticeships with painters. After moving to Amsterdam in 1631, he gained the commissions of several wealthy patrons and achieved great success. Rembrandt spent a large portion of the money he earned at auctions and his personal art collection. He encountered turbulent times both personally and financially, but he continued to produce works of art until his death in 1669.

About Art History

Most painters during the 1600s traveled to Italy to study art. Italian art and artists such as Michelangelo and Raphael were highly esteemed at this time. Rembrandt chose to remain in the Netherlands to learn about art. His remarkable ability to show feeling and emotion through dramatic lighting has made his work universally understandable and appreciated. Rembrandt is considered one of the greatest Western artists from all periods and countries.

About the Artwork

Under the painter Pieter Lastman, Rembrandt learned how to create dramatic accents using light and shadow, gesture, expression, and composition. In all, Rembrandt created more than 600 paintings as well as a large number of drawings, etchings, and more than 60 self-portraits. He most frequently created portraits, but he also completed paintings with historical, biblical, and mythological themes.

About the Media

Rembrandt worked mainly in oils on wood and canvas. He completed drawings on paper with pen and ink and also created etchings.

About the Technique

Rembrandt used a technique called *chiaroscuro,* an Italian word meaning "light and dark." He used light to focus attention on certain areas that contained details and left other parts in shadows using dark colors.

Diego Velázquez
1599–1660

Diego Velázquez (dē ā´ gō və las´ kwiz) was born in Seville, Spain, in 1599. At the young age of 11, he was apprenticed to the painter Francisco Pacheco, and by the time he was 18 he was an independent painter. In 1623, Velázquez moved to Madrid where he became court painter to King Philip IV, a comfortable position that Velázquez held until his death. Velázquez eventually became a knight of the Military Order of Santiago and a friend of the king. This occupation in court required him to paint many portraits, and his richly colored portraits captured the personalities of his subjects.

◀ **Diego Velázquez.** (Spanish).
Las Meninas (The Maids of Honor). 1656.
Oil on canvas. 10 feet $5\frac{1}{4}$ × 9 feet $\frac{3}{4}$ inches (3.18 × 2.76 m.).
Museo Nacíonnal del Prado, Madrid, Spain.

About Art History

At the beginning of his career Velázquez was influenced by *Caravaggism,* or the use of strong chiaroscuro, which includes bright light and the placement of large-scale figures in the foreground. Baroque art arrived in Europe around 1600 and was a reaction against the formulas of the mannerist style that had prevailed during the late renaissance.

About the Artwork

Complex compositions were characteristic of Velázquez's work. One of his most famous paintings is *Las Meninas (The Maids of Honor).* This multiple portrait is nearly ten-and-a-half feet tall and nine feet wide. Its illusion of space draws the viewer into the environment of the artist's studio, so the viewer is welcomed into the space occupied by King Philip and Queen Mariana, who are reflected in the large mirror in the background. The Spanish word *meninas* refers to the young court companions of the monarch's children. Velázquez depicted the young Infanta Margarita, or royal heiress to the throne, in the center of her attendants and gazing

directly at the viewer. The reflected image of her parents completes the painting as a family portrait. Velázquez also included a self-portrait in this scene. He stands to the left of Margarita with paintbrush in hand and a large canvas before him, as if he is painting a portrait of the king and queen.

About the Media

Velázquez painted with oils on canvas. Before working in Madrid, he painted figurative works set in taverns, markets, or kitchens, and still lifes of food or kitchen utensils. As a court painter he depicted historical scenes, the royal family, palace constructions, and landscapes. His increased workload serving the king required him to paint less frequently later in his career.

About the Technique

Velázquez was devoted to studying and sketching from models. He arranged his human models and still lifes with mathematical precision and was exceptionally skilled at rendering sculptural volumes and surface textures.

Jan Vermeer
1632–1675

Jan Vermeer (yän vər mer´) was a Dutch painter born in Delft. Little is known about his life; he married at the age of 21 and was the father of 11 children. Vermeer served a six-year apprenticeship and was admitted to the Delft painters guild in 1653. He made a modest living as an art dealer running a business that was left to him by his father. No records have been found to show that he sold any of his own works. Forgotten for almost 200 years, Vermeer is now regarded as one of the greatest painters of all time. This is remarkable because only 35 of his paintings are known to exist. This small number of works is attributed to his deliberate, methodical work habits, his short life, and the disappearance of many of his paintings during the period of obscurity following his death.

▲ **Jan Vermeer.** (Dutch).
Detail from *At the Procuress.* 1656.

Oil on canvas. $56\frac{3}{4} \times 51\frac{1}{8}$ inches (143 × 130 cm.).
The Dresden State Art Collection, Dresden, Germany.

About Art History

Like other Dutch artists of the seventeenth century, Vermeer painted genre scenes, landscapes, and portraits. This was different from most artwork produced in southern Europe at the time, which was primarily religious.

About the Artwork

Dutch genre painting reached its peak with Vermeer's work. He could capture a moment of life with all action seeming to cease. Vermeer masterfully depicted light and space. He usually used his wife and children as models.

About the Media

Vermeer painted with oils on canvas or wood backgrounds.

About the Technique

Vermeer was a master of optical reality. He included only the details that would be seen from a distance. His use of color and value was also consistent with what someone would actually see. He painted slowly and painstakingly, completing only two or three works a year. The textures of his painted objects are so realistic that the viewer is tempted to touch the surface to see how it feels.

Jane Wilson

b. 1924

Jane Wilson (jān wil´sən) was born on a small farm outside Seymour, Iowa, and earned degrees from the University of Iowa in Iowa City. Regarded as one of the leaders of American landscape painting, Wilson works in an abstract style that often focuses on recalling place-oriented memories and depictions of landscapes and seascapes.

About Art History

French impressionism, Dutch landscape painting, and abstract expressionism all influenced Wilson. After she moved to New York in 1949, Wilson co-founded the Hamsa Gallery and became a member of a group of artists known as the Second Generation of Abstract Expressionists. From 1947 to 1988, she was a professor at the Pratt Institute, the University of Iowa, Parsons School of Design, and Columbia University, and has been a visiting professor in eight other universities.

About the Artwork

Wilson's paintings incorporate abstract skies with low planes of land and ocean. Growing up in Iowa influenced her landscapes with their images of meadows, farmlands, flatlands, and hills, and led her to develop a strong interest in the way weather changes and acts as an event. Her paintings depict times of day and the seasons and express her meditations on time, place, weather, memory, and experience. The calm, muted appearance of *Solstice* demonstrates her meditative, intuitive approach to technique and appearance.

About the Media

Wilson paints with oil paints on finely woven linen. Her canvases are often very large, at times reaching lengths of six feet.

About the Technique

Wilson creates most of her paintings in her New York studio. Her creations do not begin with a preconceived notion of a finished product—they evolve patiently through many layers. The landscape character of her work is depicted through a series of horizontal bands of color expressing the horizon, land, water, and light. Wilson works from the top of the canvas to the bottom with a limited color palette and layer upon layer of paint, sometimes as many as 30 layers in one painting. This technique adds translucence to her work.

Headdress for Epa Masquerade

This headdress was made by an artist of the Yoruban people of Nigeria. The majority of Yoruban people today live in the west African countries of Nigeria and Benin. The exact date the headdress was created is not known, but it is estimated that it was made during the early twentieth century.

◀ **Artist unknown.** (Nigeria). *Headdress for Epa Masquerade.* c. 20th century.

Carved wood and pigment. 50 × 20 × 18 inches (127 × 50.8 × 45.72 cm.). Birmingham Museum of Art, Birmingham, Alabama.

About Art History

There are many different forms, styles, and media used in both ancient and contemporary Yoruban artwork. Pottery, textiles, weaving, beadwork, metalwork, masks, and wood carvings are some of the types of art for which the Yoruba are known. Yoruban works of art often have spiritual significance. The culture is heavily influenced by the belief in an afterworld, where ancestors live and continue to affect the lives of their descendants. Effigies and other symbols representing the deceased are still honored and displayed in Yoruban homes today.

About the Artwork

This Yoruban headdress was worn by a male dancer during the climax of the annual Epa festival, an important tradition in Yoruba culture. The Epa festival is a celebration of the various social roles of a traditional Yoruban community, including the roles of its chiefs, warriors, hunters, farmers, priests, and women. Tall, heavy, wooden masquerade masks are placed over the dancers' heads, with the bottom portion of the mask partially covering the wearer's face. Great skill is required of these dancers as they balance the heavy masks atop their heads while jumping and dancing. At one point during the Epa ceremony, a dancer must leap to the top of a mound while maintaining his balance and keeping the unwieldy headdress from falling from his head. If the dancer allows the headdress to fall, it is considered a bad omen for the community. The figure of the warrior on horseback is an image often seen on this type of Yoruban headdress, and it symbolizes the energy and authority of Yoruban warriors.

About the Technique

This headdress appears to have been carved by hand from hardwood and then painted.

Peggy Flora Zalucha
b. 1948

Peggy Flora Zalucha (peg´ ē flor´ a zə loo´ kə) was born in Peoria, Illinois. She was raised to appreciate photography and encouraged to take pictures of the world around her. When Zalucha was in college, women were not advised to get studio degrees, so Zalucha got her degree in teaching instead. Her first official job was as an art teacher in a rural Nebraska school. Zalucha has been making and teaching art for more than 20 years.

About Art History

Zalucha's paintings have been classified as modern examples of genre painting. Genre painting is the art of finding beauty in everyday life. Many of Zalucha's subjects are incorporated into traditional still-life painting styles.

About the Artwork

Zalucha's paintings are a celebration of daily life. She believes that beauty is overlooked in common things. By using watercolor paints, Zalucha feels she can unleash the jewel-like quality of her still-life paintings.

About the Media

Zalucha primarily chooses to use watercolor paints on paper. She also uses acrylic washes and India ink.

About the Technique

Zalucha feels that when she comes across new problems in her artwork, she is able to learn from her own paintings. Watercolor is a difficult medium to rework. Zalucha has developed her own style using this medium. She uses watercolor paints to allow the object she is painting to shimmer and shine. This technique makes common objects look extraordinary.

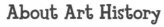

Delaware Shoulder Bag

The Indian Removal Act of 1830 forced many Native American groups to leave their homelands. The Delaware nation was pushed from homes in the Delaware and Ohio River valleys to land west of the Mississippi River. As in most Native American societies, Delaware women were responsible for caring for children, cooking, housekeeping, gardening, and creating their families' pots, baskets, and clothing.

◄ **Artist unknown** (Delaware, United States). *Delaware Shoulder Bag.* c. 1860.

Wool and cotton fabric. $8\frac{3}{5} \times 7\frac{3}{4}$ inches (21.9 × 19.7 cm.). Detroit Institute of Arts, Detroit, Michigan.

About Art History

After the Delaware's relocation to the prairies, the women combined the traditional square shape of their shoulder bags with bead embroidery. They also widened the shoulder strap. The Delaware women helped develop the "prairie style" of beadwork. They combined designs from several Native American cultures. For the *prairie style,* they filled in open areas between designs with vibrant, contrasting colors. They often created a "negative" design on the bags.

About the Artwork

Shoulder bags were worn by men at ceremonial events to show off the skills of the Delaware craftswomen.

About the Media

Delaware shoulder bags were made from wool and cotton fabric, silk ribbon, and glass beads.

About the Technique

The Delaware women used bold designs in their beadwork, placed the designs close together, and outlined them in white. The designs were abstract and symmetrical, with each side a mirror image of the other.

Gui Ritual Food Container

The ancient Chinese used bronze containers during their religious ceremonies or *rituals*. The containers were symbols of political power. The artisans who made them were well respected. Some of the containers were buried with the dead, and others were buried as offerings to the natural spirits of the rivers and mountains. Other containers were carefully hidden. When they were unearthed or found, sometimes generations later, they were treasured as links to the past. These containers now serve as a record of ancient Chinese culture and proof of the skill of its artists.

◀ **Artist unknown.** (China). *Gui Ritual Food Container.* Zhou Dynasty, 11th century B.C.

Bronze. Arthur M. Sackler Gallery, Smithsonian Institution, Washington, D.C.

About Art History

The Bronze Age in China lasted nearly 1,000 years. Each period of the Bronze Age produced a variety of styles of containers. Each style has a different name, characteristic, and purpose. There are more than 100 styles of containers from the Bronze Age. The first ancient ritual food container was offered for sale in the early twentieth century and was probably produced during the eleventh century B.C.

About the Artwork

Ancient bronze containers were shaped to suit their functions. In addition to the round, wide-mouthed ritual food containers there were narrow-necked wine containers and shallow water basins. Many of the bronze containers produced during the Western Zhou period, from 1050 to 771 B.C., were decorated with images of long-tailed birds that looked like peacocks. Later these birds were stylized and became bands of patterns that circled the container. Long inscriptions on some of the containers recorded important historical information.

About the Media

This container was made of bronze.

About the Technique

By the time of the Western Zhou dynasty, artisans no longer created containers by beating cold bronze into shape. Instead they made a mold from clay and carved the design they wanted into it. Then they poured molten bronze into the mold. When it cooled, the container needed only polishing.

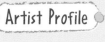

Indonesian Shadow Puppet

Indonesia is a country in southeast Asia that consists of more than 13,600 islands. The islands lie along the equator and extend more than 3,000 miles. Indonesia ranks fifth in population among all countries. The most famous art forms of Indonesia include dances of the old royal courts of Java and the dramatic folk dances of Bali. Puppet dramas are a major part of Javanese and Balinese cultures. The most popular puppets are flat and made of leather.

▲ **Artist unknown.** (Indonesian).
Indonesian Shadow Puppet. c. 1950.

Cut, painted leather. 31$\frac{1}{2}$ inches (80.01 cm.) high.
Private Collection.

About Art History

Shadow theatre is part of the general development of theatre in southeast Asia. The first theatre consisted of characters drawn on long sheets of paper. A puppeteer, called the *dalang,* unrolled the paper as he told the story. During the fifteenth century shadow theatre became children's entertainment. About that time the moving shadow puppets were developed to tell religious stories. More recent theatre uses masked human actors in place of puppets. The audience watches the actors, not their shadows.

About the Artwork

One type of shadow theatre takes place outdoors. Shadows from the puppets are projected onto a long screen. The light is often provided by a flickering oil lamp. The *dalang* sits in front of the screen, in view of the men in the audience. The women sit on the other side of the screen and watch the shadows. Musicians accompany the story, which can last more than one night. One example of shadow theatre is "The Story of Arayana," a story of love and revenge among the ancient rajahs.

About the Media

Some early shadow puppets were made from thin wood or buffalo skin carved into intricate designs. In time, rounded puppets that looked more like humans became popular. These puppets wore elaborately carved, painted, or printed costumes. The shadow puppets were usually princes, sages, apes, officers, or clowns.

Leopard Aquamanile

This aquamanile was made by an unknown artist of the Edo people of the Court of Benin. The majority of Edo people today live in the neighboring nations of Benin and Nigeria in west Africa. The artistic and cultural traditions of these people have been well maintained through the years to the present day. The word *aquamanile* refers to a hollow vessel used to pour water for washing the hands.

◄ **Artist unknown,** Court of Benin. (Nigeria). *Leopard Aquamanile.* 16th–19th century.
••
Brass. $7\frac{7}{8}$ inches (20 cm.).
The Metropolitan Museum of Art, New York, New York.

About Art History

One Edo legend tells of how the revered leader Oba Ewuare the Great, who ruled the Court of Benin during the fifteenth century, took beautiful brass aquamaniles and other vessels from Olokun, the god of the sea. Because Ewuare believed these brass objects had magical powers bestowed upon them by Olokun's father, Osanobua, the creator god in Beninese mythology, he placed them on the state shrine in his palace. Legends such as this one led to a traditional Edo belief that brass containers such as this aquamanile house spirits that communicate through sounds that emanate from inside the vessels. Aquamaniles and other brass containers are still used to carry water and ceremonial items during rituals and spiritual celebrations performed by Edo people today.

About the Artwork

In Benin and neighboring Nigeria, aquamaniles were often created in the form of leopards, the beast regarded as the most powerful, ferocious, and regal of local animals. This aquamanile has holes in the nostril area where water can be dispensed for hand washing during, or in preparation for, a tribal ceremony honoring the ancestral leader Ewuare. Because the aquamanile is meant only for this special purpose, it is stored on a sacred altar to Ewuare when not in use.

About the Media

This aquamanile is made of brass, an alloy of the elemental metals copper and zinc.

About the Technique

This aquamanile was created by brasscasting, a popular method used in Benin and Nigeria for creating aquamaniles and other types of vessels. Some oral histories of the region claim that the art of brasscasting was first practiced in the fourteenth century A.D. after it was introduced by brasscasters from the Yoruban culture.

Lekythos

Attributed to the Amasis Painter

The Amasis Painter was a celebrated artist in ancient Greece who is best known for his decoration of pottery. His title comes from the name of the Greek potter, Amasis, who made at least eight Attic Black-figure vases. The Amasis Painter adorned many ceramic objects with his beautifully detailed artwork, and more than 130 of these pieces have been preserved.

◀ **Attributed to the Amasis Painter.** (Greek). *Lekythos (oil flask).* c. 550–530 B.C.

The Metropolitan Museum of Art, New York, New York.

About Art History

This work was made during the Archaic period in Greek history, which lasted from 700 to 480 B.C. It was a period of great invention and creative expression in ancient Greece, a time when the subject matter of sculptures and paintings truly reflected Greek society and ideals. Artists of this era were fascinated with the study and portrayal of the human figure. Many beautifully realistic images of men and women appeared in works of sculpture, pottery, paintings, and friezes. Vase painting, such as that done by the Amasis Painter, was an important art form in ancient Greece. Many art historians believe that it was during the Archaic period that vase painting reached its height.

About the Artwork

This lekythos is a ceramic oil flask created by the Amasis Potter during the sixth century, B.C. in Athens, Greece. It is classified as a *Black-figure* work of pottery because of the style and color of the images painted on its surface. This oil flask is covered with images of a seated woman, four young men, eight dancing maidens, and several women engaged in various activities related to spinning and preparing wool cloth. The skill of the artist is evident in the realistic proportions of the women and the fine detail included in the scene.

About the Media

This lekythos is made of painted terra-cotta ceramic.

Maison Carrée

The large stone temple *Maison Carrée* was built during the first century, B.C. under the direction of Marcus Vipsanius Agrippa, the son-in-law of the Roman emperor Augustus. *Maison Carree* means "square house" in French.

◀ **Artist unknown.** (France).
Maison Carrée. c. First century B.C.
Limestone. Nimes, France.

About Art History

The Roman emperor Augustus reigned in the early Empire period, which lasted from 27 B.C. until 180 A.D. Augustus established impressive urban centers in the Roman provinces. One of the most amazing accomplishments of the Roman engineers is the Pont du Gard, also located in Nimes, France. This enormous, 180-foot-tall bridge was originally designed to serve as an aqueduct. This aqueduct was so well planned, designed, and built that it was able to supply each person in the city of Nimes with 100 gallons of water every day.

About the Artwork

The city of Nimes, located in the Provence region in southern France, was under Roman control at the time *Maison Carrée* was built. The architects and builders of the temple were Roman, and the design and composition of the structure are characteristically Roman. The style of *Maison Carrée* is classified as *Roman Provincial Corinthian.* Earlier Etruscan temples inspired this style, which is characteristic of Roman architecture. The frieze around *Maison Carrée,* taken from the Ara Pacis in Rome, is an excellent example of the Augustan Classical style.

About the Media

Maison Carrée was made from blocks of cut limestone.

About the Technique

Stonemasons cut precisely measured stones to build *Maison Carrée.* The methods used to build the temple were technologically advanced for the time, and are still impressive today. *Maison Carrée* is similar in design to the temple dedicated to Portunus in Rome, but it is actually larger and more grandly decorated than the original.

Map Quilt

This quilt was made by an unidentified American artist in 1886. Although it is not known who created the quilt, it is believed the quilt may have been made by a group of women at a quilting bee or quilting party, the process of completing the piece would have been quite time consuming.

▲ **Artist unknown.** (American). *Map Quilt.* 1886.

Silk and cotton with silk embroidery.
$78\frac{3}{4} \times 82\frac{1}{4}$ inches. (200.03 × 208.92 cm.).
American Museum of Folk Art, New York, New York.

About Art History

Quilt making as an art form has been important to American culture over the past few centuries. Not only have quilts been made for the practical purpose of keeping people warm, they have been embroidered with names, dates, images, and symbols of the histories of individual families and the country itself. Some quilts commemorate an important event in the history of a state or town, and others feature beautifully designed family trees where the names and birth dates of new generations are added over the years.

About the Artwork

This quilt was probably made to serve as a bedspread. Quilts featuring elaborate designs and beautiful stitching and embroidery were often made as wedding gifts, baby gifts, or as friendship quilts.

About the Media

This quilt was made from many small pieces of colored silk and cotton fabric, and was sewn and detailed with silk embroidery thread.

About the Technique

All patchwork quilts are assembled in a similar way, although infinite patterns, designs, styles, and sewing techniques are used to create them. The construction begins with many small scraps and cuttings of fabric. These scraps are cut into the desired shapes (in this case the shapes of individual states) then stitched together from the underside of the quilt's top layer. When the top layer of stitching is complete, a bottom layer is sewn to the top, and batting, fiber filling, or feathers are sewn into the middle layer. Finish stitching keeps the stuffing from shifting within the finished quilt. This quilt was finished with decorative topstitching.

Pectoral with the Name of Senwosret II

Artists of the Middle Kingdom of ancient Egypt are known for their skilled attention to even the smallest detail. Artists of this period demonstrated more freedom of creative expression than those of earlier periods, creating ornately beautiful works of precious metals, stone, granite, wood, plaster, gesso, and ceramics. Middle Kingdom jewelers created spectacular ornaments for the royalty who wore them.

▲ **Artist unknown** (Egypt). *Pectoral with the Name of Senwosret II.* C. 1897–1878 B.C.

Gold, carnelian, feldspar, garnet, turquoise.
Length of pectoral $3\frac{1}{4}$ inches (8.25 cm.).
The Metropolitan Museum of Art, New York, New York.

About Art History

This pectoral was found at el-Lahun, Egypt, in the funerary complex of King Senwosret II. Because a belief in an afterworld and rebirth after earthly death dominated much of ancient Egyptian cultural tradition, it is not surprising that artwork created by this culture depicted and celebrated life in an afterworld. Sculptures, household objects, food, currency, and ornaments such as this pectoral were buried in the tombs of deceased rulers, the belief being that these items would be needed in the afterworld.

About the Artwork

A pectoral is a large piece of jewelry worn on the upper chest, over the area of the pectorals below the collarbone. This pectoral, made for and worn by Egyptian King Senwosret II, bears the symbols, images, and hieroglyphs of a complex written language, used here to spell out his name and the message "May the sun god give eternal life to Senwosret II." Some of the symbols are recognizable as falcons, cobras, a sun, a scarab beetle, a man, and palm fronds. Each image and symbol must be interpreted to decipher the complete message.

About the Media

This pectoral was made from gold and several different types of semiprecious stones.

About the Technique

The gold parts of the pectoral were formed from molten gold, then carved and polished. The semiprecious stones were carved into delicate forms and precisely fitted into the gold portions.

Plate with King Hunting Rams

Many artists were skilled in metalwork in fifth- and sixth-century Persia, located in what is modern-day Iran. The name of the metalsmith who created this dish is not known. Because the style and techniques used to make this plate were widely practiced during this time period in Persia, the work of this particular artist cannot be isolated as a means of identifying him.

◀ **Artist unknown.** (Iran). *Plate with King Hunting Rams.* Late fifth century A.D.
••
Silver with mercury gilding and niello inlay. Diameter 8⅝ inches (21.9 cm.). The Metropolitan Museum of Art, New York, New York.

About Art History

During the Sassanian period of Persian history, the depiction of royalty engaged in the act of hunting wild beasts became a popular theme in works of art. Celebrating the bravery and skill of a king was so important to a royal family that they even commissioned plates to be made with these magnificent images and sent them to members of neighboring courts as gifts.

About the Artwork

The exact identity of the Sassanian king featured on this plate is not known. Symbols on the crown indicate that this king may have been either Peroz, who ruled from 459 A.D. to 484 A.D., or Kavad, who ruled from 488 A.D. to 497 A.D.

About the Media

This plate was made primarily from silver, gold, mercury, and a silver and sulfur alloy called *niello*.

About the Technique

The technique used to create this plate was typical of the Sassanian period. Silver was hammered into the form of the plate, with grooves and tiny flaps cut into its front surface to receive inlays. The sculpted silver forms of the king, horse, and rams were then inserted and secured by the grooves and flaps, resulting in pronounced relief images. These images were gilded with gold and mercury, and the niello was inlaid. This complex process resulted in beautiful variations of color, texture, and contour.

Princess Feather and Rising Sun Quilt

This American quilt was made in Newark, New Jersey, during the mid-1800s. Although little is known about the quilter, it may be assumed that Catherine Fitzgerald was from a relatively prosperous American family. When this quilt was made, nearly all quiltmakers were women. Considering the amount of time needed to design, cut, assemble, and sew a quilt, the maker was someone who had significant time to spend on these tasks, free from other work.

▲ **Catherine Fitzgerald.** (United States).
Princess Feather and Rising Sun Quilt.
c. 1840–1850.
•••
Cotton pieced and appliquéd. 102 × 93 inches (259.08 × 236.22 cm.)
Collection of the Newark Museum, Newark, New Jersey.

About Art History

American women are world renowned for the unique and beautiful quilts they design and sew by hand. These quilts are so well-made that if they are gently used and cared for they can be passed down through many generations as family heirlooms. In many American communities, quilts have traditionally been made and given as gifts for special occasions such as weddings and the birth of children.

About the Artwork

The *Princess Feather and Rising Sun* quilt was probably made to serve as a bedspread. Quilts featuring elaborate designs and beautiful stitching and embroidery were often made as wedding gifts, baby gifts, or as "friendship quilts" to be given to friends or family as remembrances in the event of their relocation to a new area.

About the Media

This quilt was made from small pieces of colored cotton fabric and was sewn with cotton thread. Because cotton is durable, stands up well to repeated laundering, and does not decay as quickly as other quilting media such as silk and velvet, most of the remaining quilts from the mid-nineteenth century are those made of cotton.

About the Technique

Most patchwork quilts are assembled in a similar way, although infinite patterns, designs, styles, and sewing techniques are used to create individual quilts. The construction of a quilt like the one shown here begins with small cuttings of fabric. When the quilt design and pattern have been determined, these fabric pieces are cut into the desired shapes, and then appliquéd to the quilt's top layer.

Pueblo Scene: Corn Dancers and Church

A Pueblo Indian artist from New Mexico created the miniatures that make up *Pueblo Scene: Corn Dancers and Church.* It is estimated that the piece was made in 1960. This type of earthenware sculpture work was common in the region where the piece was made.

▲ **Vigil Family. (Pueblo).** (United States). *Pueblo Scene: Corn Dancers and Church.* 1960.

Painted earthenware.
Museum of International Folk Art, Santa Fe, New Mexico.

About Art History

Corn dances are part of Pueblo Indian ceremonies and are performed as prayers or requests for rain and bountiful harvests. The rituals of Pueblo Indians have been important to their culture for many centuries. When the Spanish introduced the Roman Catholic religion to the people of the Americas in the sixteenth century, some groups assimilated Catholicism into their traditional religious beliefs, ceremonies, and cultural traditions. It is common for the religious imagry seen in Mexican, Central and South American, Carribbean, and southwestern American art to contain elements of both traditional religions and Roman Catholicism.

About the Artwork

The scene depicted in *Pueblo Scene: Corn Dancers and Church* is not an exact reenactment of a Pueblo corn dance ceremony. It is a creative interpretation of several kinds of Pueblo Indian celebrations, rituals, and ceremonies combined into one impressionistic scene. The event shown by the sculpture is centered around a feast, with ceremonial corn dancers and masked Kachina dancers in attendance.

About the Media

This scene was made from clay and paint.

About the Technique

The exact technique used to create this scene is not known, but the figures that make up the piece appear to have been formed by hand, dried and baked in a kiln, and then painted.

Shadow Puppet

It is not known exactly who created this puppet, but the quality and care with which was made indicate that it was skillfully designed and crafted using traditional methods.

◀ **Artist unknown.** (Thailand). *Shadow Puppet.*
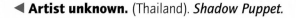
Cut and painted leather. 25 inches (63.5 cm.) tall.
The Yoshida Collection.

About Art History

Shadow puppets are one of the more recognizable forms of traditional Thai art. These unique works have evolved over many years from plain, simple cutout patterns to the colorful, ornate, fascinating characters displayed in shops and museums all over Thailand today. The shadow puppet shown here is a good example of a beautiful and exotic piece created by a skilled Thai puppet master.

About the Artwork

This puppet might have been created as part of the puppet cast of a traditional *Nang Talung,* the original shadow puppet theater of southern Thailand. During a Nang Talung, puppet masters move their shadow puppets from behind a back-lit white curtain, narrating the play and providing the voices for the various characters. Performing all of these tasks simultaneously requires a great deal of talent. Shadow puppets are still popular at festivals, birthdays, and other types of celebrations.

About the Media

Traditional Thai shadow puppets are made of treated leather, paint, and bamboo rods.

About the Technique

The basic method used to make Thai shadow puppets is complex. To begin the process, a treated leather hide is stretched and dried on a wooden frame. After the leather has stiffened and dried, an artist draws the puppet design on the leather. Using small hand tools, the artist painstakingly cuts out the puppet form. This cutting step can take hours, days, weeks, or even longer, depending on the intricacy of the puppet being created. After the leather portion of the puppet is cut, movable parts are created by fastening parts of the puppet together with rivets or string. The puppet is then painted in the traditional colors of red, green, yellow, and black. Finally, bamboo rods are attached at pivotal points, enabling the puppeteer to manipulate the shadow puppet.